Denied A Mummy

THE HEARTBREAKING STORY OF THREE LITTLE CHILDREN SEARCHING FOR SOMEONE TO LOVE THEM

MAGGIE HARTLEY

First published in 2018 by Trapeze,
an imprint of The Orion Publishing Group Ltd
Carmelite House, 50 Victoria Embankment,
London EC4Y 0DZ

An Hachette UK company

1 3 5 7 9 10 8 6 4 2

ISBN (Paperback): 978 1 409 17709 8
ISBN (eBook): 978 1 409 17710 4

Typeset by Born Group

Denied A Mummy

Also by Maggie Hartley

Dedication

This book is dedicated to Mary, Sean, Dougie and Louisa, all the children and teenagers who have passed through my home, and the children who live with me now. It's been a privilege to have cared for you and to be able to share your stories. Thank you for your determination, strength and joy and for sharing your lives with me.

Contents

A Message from Maggie

I wanted to write this book to give people an honest account about what it's like to be a foster carer, to talk about some of the challenges that I face on a day-to-day basis and some of the children that I've helped.

My main concern is to protect the children that have been in my care. For this reason all names and identifying details have been changed, including my own, and no locations have been included. But I can assure you that all my stories are based on real-life cases from my own experiences.

Being a foster carer is a privilege and I couldn't imagine doing anything else. My house is never quiet but I wouldn't have it any other way. I hope perhaps my stories will inspire other people to consider fostering as new carers are always desperately needed.

Maggie Hartley

ONE

Wild Creatures

During my many years as a foster carer I've seen shocking things and been exposed to some of the very worst suffering that children can possibly endure. But despite my years of experience, my heart broke when I saw the three little figures standing on my doorstep. They looked more like wild animals than children. They all had the same long, matted brown hair hanging in dreadlocks around their gaunt little faces, and their skin was thick with grime. This wasn't just ordinary dirt but the kind of ingrained filth that seeps into every pore and takes endless baths to get out. Their clothes were so mucky and worn it was impossible to make out what colour they were supposed to be. To be honest, I couldn't even tell whether they were girls or boys.

They cowered behind the social worker, their bodies quivering and their eyes wide with fear. I crouched down so I was on their level. As I got closer to them, the overpowering stench of faeces made my nostrils tingle.

'Hello, I'm Maggie,' I said gently, smiling. 'Come on in.'

The smallest one, who couldn't have been older than four or five and I guessed was a little boy, made a hacking sound in his throat. I flinched as a glob of phlegm flew out of his mouth and landed on my cheek.

'I told you no spitting,' the social worker reprimanded him.

He snarled at her like an angry animal.

'I'm sorry,' she said apologetically, rummaging in her bag and handing me a tissue. 'I'm afraid they're a bit of a lively bunch.'

As I wiped the sticky mucus off my cheek, I had a feeling that that was a bit of an understatement.

'I'm Lisa Middleton by the way,' she told me, shaking my hand. 'Their social worker.'

She was very young and I could only assume that she was newly qualified. She looked dishevelled, exhausted and to be honest, completely out of her depth. She was dressed as if she was going to a business meeting. The cream blouse that she was wearing was covered in all sorts of dirty marks and smears and her black pencil skirt and heels were totally unsuitable for chasing these three children round.

'It's been a complete nightmare getting them here,' she sighed. 'I strapped them all in their car seats and within minutes they'd undone their buckles. I probably stopped twenty times on the way from the hospital to here.'

'Come in and we can have a chat,' I told her.

Thankfully, the three children obediently trooped into the house, looking around nervously.

Like so many of my placements, the children had arrived with virtually no warning. An hour ago I was reading through some notes on a recent training session that I'd done when I'd got a call from Becky, my supervising social worker from the fostering agency that I worked for, to ask if I was willing to take three siblings who had just been removed from a house by police. At this stage, I knew nothing else about these children and had no idea how long they might be with me.

'Who have we got here then?' I asked Lisa. 'I don't even know anyone's names.'

'This is Mary, who is eight,' she said, gesturing to the tallest child.

Mary looked at me blankly, her wide blue eyes devoid of any emotion.

'And this is Sean who's seven, and five-year-old Dougie,' she added.

So despite the long brown hair, the younger two were boys. They both scowled at me.

'I think they might be hungry,' Lisa told me. 'They've been at the hospital being checked over for a couple of hours so they haven't had anything to eat.'

It was 5 p.m. by now – the time I'd normally give younger kids their tea.

'OK then,' I said cheerfully. 'Let's go through to the kitchen and I'll sort you something out.'

Lisa herded the children down the hall and into the kitchen where they cowered in a corner.

'I think I'll do you what I like to call a fridge picnic,' I told them cheerfully.

They stared blankly back at me.

A fridge picnic was good for putting something together quickly at short notice and consisted of a few bits that I always had ready in the fridge. It was simple to eat and that way the children could choose the food that they liked.

I rummaged in the fridge and got some things together – a pile of bread and some butter and jam, a packet of Babybels, slices of ham, some cucumber, carrots and yogurts. Three pairs of eyes watched warily as I carried the tray of food to the kitchen table.

As soon as I put it down, the children ran towards it like a pack of hungry wolves, pushing and shoving each other out of the way in a desperate bid to get to it first. I'd put some plastic plates and knives and forks out but they ignored those and crammed as much as they could into their mouths. Sean grabbed a handful of ham and half the loaf of bread and scuttled off into a corner. Dougie meanwhile was so desperate to get to the food he stood up on a chair and climbed onto the table. He shoved his hand into the jar of jam and started scooping fistfuls of it into his mouth. I ran over to him and lifted him back down.

'We sit on chairs in this house, sweetheart, not the table,' I told him gently.

I knew this wasn't the time to start insisting on manners but I didn't want him to fall. He quickly grabbed a handful of Babybels, crawled under the table and started eating them. Mary meanwhile had pulled open all the yogurts and was shovelling them into her mouth with her filthy fingers.

'You were right about them being hungry,' I said, raising my eyes at Lisa, who was watching this spectacle with a look of absolute horror on her face.

With the huge amounts they were cramming into their mouths and the speed at which they were doing it, I was more worried that they were going to make themselves sick.

'I think I'll clear some of it away otherwise they'll be ill,' I told her quietly.

I was putting the lid back on the jam when Sean ran over to me.

'No b**ch,' he hissed. 'I want that.'

Before I could say anything he grabbed the jar out of my hand and kicked me hard in the shin. I grimaced as a sharp pain seared through the front of my leg.

'No kicking, Sean,' I told him firmly. 'We don't kick people in this house.'

He growled at me and ran into a corner with the jar.

'Are you OK, Maggie?' gasped Lisa. 'He lashed out at me a few times on the way here.'

'Yep,' I said, giving my leg a rub. 'I think I'll live.'

It was never nice when a child hurt you but this definitely wasn't the first time and I knew it wasn't going to be the last. I knew why Sean had done it. It was obvious that food had been in short supply at their house and they had that survival instinct that many neglected children have to grab food when they can because they don't know when they'll next have any. I'd realised by now that I'd made completely the wrong decision by putting a choice of food out and letting them help themselves.

Once they'd eaten, the children seemed to develop a second wind. Dougie leapt onto the sofa and threw all the cushions off. He ran over to the patio doors and swung off the curtains leaving them smeared with dirt and jam.

'Out, out, out,' he grunted, banging the plastic beaker he had in his hand against the glass.

'You can't go outside now, sweetie,' I told him. 'I need to talk to Lisa.'

Meanwhile Mary and Sean had gone over to the toy cupboard and were proceeding to open up every drawer and empty out all the contents. There were bits of Lego every-where and Sean was tipping jigsaws and board games out of their boxes one by one.

Normally I wouldn't talk to a social worker about a child in front of them but with these three, I had no choice. I could see from their behaviour so far that I couldn't risk leaving them alone in another room. So, as difficult as it was, I had to try and turn a blind eye to the chaos they were causing while I got as much information as possible from Lisa.

'So what can you tell me?' I asked her in a low voice.

She quietly explained that earlier in the day the police had carried out a drugs raid on a flat.

'Neighbours had complained about people coming and going at all hours and they suspected drug dealing was going on there,' she told me. 'When the police raided the place they said it was like a squat – mattresses everywhere, people passed out, piles of rubbish and flies everywhere.

'The police thought they had dogs because the floor was absolutely covered with piles of excrement and the flat stank,' she continued. 'They assumed the dogs had been trapped inside and had gone to the toilet wherever they wished.

'Then they realised that there were no dogs. It was these three children.'

'Oh my good God,' I sighed, appalled by the horrors these three siblings had been exposed to. 'Poor little mites.'

I looked over at them. Dougie was kicking the glass and Sean was throwing cushions at him. Only Mary was sitting quietly, surrounded by the pile of toys that had been emptied out of the cupboard.

It was no wonder they behaved like this if they had been left to fend for themselves.

'How did this happen?' I asked Lisa. 'Had they dropped off Social Service's radar?'

'Unbelievably, they'd never been on it,' she replied. 'We didn't even know these kids existed. No one did.'

She described how there was a record of Mary in Ireland where she had been born. At some stage the family had come over to England and since then, they'd moved around the country every few months.

'The boys don't have any documents,' she explained. 'They're not registered with any GPs. None of them have ever been to school. From what we can gather, their parents spent their days shoplifting to pay for their drug habit while the kids were left to fend for themselves.'

All I could think was that it was a miracle that three small children had managed to survive in that environment for so long.

'I can see they're scrawny but it's a wonder they're not in a worse state,' I sighed.

'They have been fed,' sighed Lisa. 'Probably on whatever their parents managed to steal. Lots of biscuits, crisps, chocolate and the odd bit of bread by the sound of it. They're very thin and pale but amazingly not too underweight. The hospital also found they've got fleas.'

Lisa explained their parents Kathleen and Darren had been arrested for possession, supply and child endangerment.

'They were both completely out of it when the police raided the flat,' she said. 'Neither of them had a clue what was going on.'

'Did the children bring anything with them?' I asked.

Lisa shook her head.

'Believe me, you wouldn't have wanted anything from there, Maggie,' she sighed. 'It would be cruel to even keep an animal in those conditions. Everything stank and was covered in dirt, urine, faeces or flies so there was no way I was about to start sorting through it.'

As Lisa was talking, I glanced over at Dougie and realised that, much to my horror, he'd pulled his trousers down and was starting to wee on the floor.

'No, flower,' I said, rushing over to him. 'You need to wee in the toilet. Come on, let me show you where it is.'

But the puddle on the laminate told me that it was too late for that.

'They've never been toilet-trained so they're used to peeing and pooing wherever they want,' Lisa told me apologetically.

I couldn't be angry with Dougie because I knew that it wasn't his fault. The level of cruelty and neglect that these poor children had endured was horrendous. It was enough to make me cry. It was no wonder they were feral. They'd been left to fend for themselves and run wild while their parents were off their heads on drugs. They'd had no boundaries or rules, no love or affection. Their short lives had instead been a constant battle for survival.

By now, the two boys had both turned their attention to my Welsh dresser. Sean was emptying out the drawers and Dougie had climbed up onto it and was in reaching distance of all my crockery. I knew I had to intervene before he hurt himself or something got smashed.

'Please don't climb up there, Dougie, it's dangerous,' I told him.

He struggled in my arms and as I lifted him down, he sunk his teeth into my hand.

'No,' I said firmly. 'No biting.'

Amidst all the chaos I noticed Lisa glance at her watch. I could tell that she couldn't wait to get out and away from these three unruly children.

'I'm so sorry, Maggie, but I've got to get going now,' she told me apologetically. 'There's some paperwork I need to do back at the office.

'I'm sure they'll calm down eventually,' she said, giving me a weak smile.

I wasn't so convinced.

'Children, I'm going to go now but Maggie will look after you and I'll give her a ring in the morning to see how you're getting on,' she told them as she hurriedly gathered up her bag.

None of them were listening to a word she said and seemed oblivious to her leaving.

As I walked into the hallway with her, I heard her tut.

'Oh damn, my tights are laddered,' she sighed. 'They were new on this morning.'

I smiled as sympathetically as I could, but inside I couldn't help but think that three feral children were trashing my kitchen and here she was worried about her tights.

'I'll give you a ring tomorrow to see how it's all going,' she told me, smiling grimly.

'Thanks,' I replied, quickly closing the door and hurrying back to see what was going on in the kitchen.

I walked back in to find the boys having a cushion fight with each other. Mary had opened up the cupboards and was pulling all of my baking stuff out.

'Right then,' I told them. 'This is what's going to happen now. We're all going to go upstairs to the bathroom.'

When children come to me in this kind of a state there's only one place I can start. I knew I needed to get them all in the bath and try to start getting them clean.

As I herded them upstairs, Mary looked apprehensive. She was a lot calmer than her younger brothers and kept glancing at me nervously.

'Mary, do you want to help me to give your brothers a bath first and then you can have one afterwards?' I asked her.

She stared at me, a terrified look in her eyes.

'A bath?' she replied in a tiny voice, a puzzled look on her face. 'We ain't had one of them for a long time. Our one was broken.'

'I'll make it nice and bubbly for you,' I told her.

'Will it hurt?' she asked.

I smiled.

'No, flower, it won't hurt,' I said. 'It'll be lovely warm water so you can get nice and clean.'

Once I'd got them into the bathroom and the bath was running, I knew I needed to get the boys undressed. Some foster carers put on rubber gloves when they're undressing children or changing nappies. While I understand why they do that, it was something I could never bring myself to do with my foster children. I knew if I had my own children I wouldn't use gloves to change them and I didn't want these kids to think that I saw them as disgusting. The sad fact was that the stench coming from the children was over-powering, but luckily, over the years I'd become an expert in mouth-breathing.

I pulled out the plastic changing mat and got Dougie to lie down on it so I could quickly pull his clothes off. He was wearing a girl's tracksuit bottoms that were far too small, so they looked like shorts on him, and a tiny faded t-shirt that was also meant for a toddler.

His little body was wiry and pale. His translucent skin was covered in scabs and fleabites and his nails were thick with a crust of dirt.

As I peeled his pants off I could see he had done a poo in them and his bottom was red and sore and encrusted with dried faeces.

'Nearly done,' I said gently.

Once his clothes were off, I put them into a carrier bag that I'd discreetly put in the bin later.

I carefully lifted him into the bath and saw him flinch as his sore skin hit the water, which immediately started turning a murky shade of brown.

Then I turned to Sean.

'Can you take your own clothes off or do you want me to help you?' I asked him gently.

He didn't say anything, he just snarled at me.

'Come on then, I'll give you a hand,' I said.

Before he could object, I'd quickly pulled his clothes off too. They were all way too small and ripped and holey. Like Dougie, his skin was red-raw and his trousers and pants were soaked with urine. I lifted him into the bath and as his body hit the water, he started to scream. Loud, ear-piercing screams.

'I don't think he likes the washing thing,' said Mary, backing away from the bath and looking equally as terrified as her little brother.

'It's OK, Sean,' she whispered, trying to soothe him. 'The lady says you just need to get clean.'

It was sweet to see her trying to comfort her brother even though she was unsure herself.

'Your sister's right,' I told him gently. 'I know it's sore, lovey, but I need to give you a wash and get you nice and clean. Then you'll feel much better.'

I quickly got out the bucket of bath toys and tried to distract him.

'Look at all these things,' I said cheerfully. 'There are boats and whales and wind-up mermaids.'

Thankfully it did the trick. Sean stopped screaming and soon the two boys were throwing bath toys at each other. It was like trying to contain two wriggling fish. As they leapt around in the bath, the water sloshed over the side soaking the floor, but it didn't matter. My priority was to get them as clean as I could.

It's no easy job trying to remove weeks or even months of ingrained dirt. I put some soap on a flannel and washed them both as gently and as quickly as I could.

'Let's do your nails now,' I told them. 'I've got a special brush that will get them nice and clean.'

They both watched mesmerised as I got the nailbrush out and scrubbed at the thick crust of dirt under their nails. Afterwards I shampooed their hair, rinsing it with jugs of fresh water and attempted to untangle the mess of knots with some detangling spray. Thankfully by this stage, both of the boys were calm. They seemed to like the feeling of being in the warm water and both of them were intrigued by what I was doing. The peace didn't last for long, though.

I knew it was time to get them out when Sean started tipping bottles of shower gel and shampoo into the bath.

When they came out they looked cleaner and they smelt a bit fresher but I knew it was going to take several more soaks before they would be properly clean. At least it was a start and I'd got enough surface grime off to make them more comfortable.

After I'd dried them both, I put a pull-up on each of them.

'What's that?' Sean scowled, tugging at the elastic.

'It's just so you don't have to worry about where the toilet is for now,' I told him gently. 'When you can show me that you can do wees and poos in the toilet, then you can wear pants.'

Lisa had told me they'd never been toilet-trained and I couldn't just have them going to the toilet wherever they wanted, like they had at home.

As the murky brown water drained out of the bath, I took a deep breath and steeled myself for round two. Two children down, one to go. The three of them had only been here just over an hour and already I was totally and utterly exhausted by these traumatised children. My heart went out to them for the terrible things that they'd been through, but at the same time I couldn't help but feel worried. What on earth had I taken on?

TWO

Bath and Bed Battle

After I'd cleaned out the bath and got rid of the thick coating of scum, I filled it up again for Mary. I helped Sean and Dougie get dressed into some pyjamas, then I took them into my bedroom. As soon as we walked in, they launched themselves onto my bed and started rolling around.

'I'm going to put on a DVD for you both while I sort your sister out,' I told them, desperately hoping that it would be enough to keep them quiet and distracted for a few minutes.

I had a portable DVD player in one of my drawers that had a Peppa Pig DVD in it. I knew it was probably a bit young for these two and I prayed it would be enough to stop them wreaking havoc while I sorted out their sister.

'It's going to come on any second now,' I told them anxiously as the two boys began wrestling each other.

Finally, the screen flickered into life and thankfully the pair of them were instantly glued to it. The effect of TV on some children never ceases to amaze me. You can have the most energetic, boisterous child but as soon as you put them in front of a screen it's as if they go into a trance.

People have different opinions about using screens to keep children quiet. I believe there's a time and a place for them and this certainly was it. I needed to know that the boys were going to be safe while I sorted out Mary and also that my bedroom wasn't going to get trashed. As an extra precaution, I also closed the stairgate at the top of the stairs so they couldn't go downstairs without me.

I went back into the bathroom where Mary was standing nervously, looking at the bath toys.

'Do you think you can get yourself undressed, sweetie?' I asked her and she nodded shyly.

While she took off the holey t-shirt and the filthy leggings she was wearing, I rummaged around in the cupboard and found a glittery bath bomb.

'I'll put this in the bath for you,' I told her. 'It will make the water all nice and sparkly.'

I also fished out a pink flannel and some Disney Princess shower gel. Her skin wasn't as sore as the boys', but it was just as translucent and she was also covered in bites. All of the children's skin was dry and hardened as if it had toughened up to cope with the levels of dirt.

Unlike her brothers, Mary got into the bath without making a fuss. I distracted her with the bath toys while I shampooed her hair and tried to detangle it with spray and a comb. It was so badly matted I knew it was going to take a few attempts and probably a haircut to deal with all the knots.

'You've got such beautiful long hair,' I told her. 'Do you like bows and clips?'

'Don't know.' She shrugged. 'Never had none.'

'I'm sure I've got a basket of hair accessories somewhere that I can try and dig out for you. Would you like that?'

She nodded.

'What's your favourite colour?' I asked her as I worked on a particularly big tangle at the back of her head.

'Can't remember,' she said, chewing her lip.

'Well, I've got all sorts of colours of bows and bobbles so you'll be able to choose your favourite,' I told her. 'I've got pink and purple, red and yellow, stripy ones and spotty ones.'

I gave her a flannel and squirted some of the shower gel on it.

'Do you think you could give yourself a wash while I go and check on your brothers?' I asked her.

She nodded. I dashed across the landing to my bedroom, nervous of what I was about to find. Thankfully the boys were still sitting on the bed together, glued to the DVD player. My heart leapt when I heard Mary calling out to me.

'Maggie, Maggie!' she yelled.

I ran back into the bathroom in a panic.

'Look,' she told me, beaming at me. 'My arms are all sparkly.'

I smiled back at her, moved at how much she was enjoying being in the bath.

When she got out I handed her a towel and showed her how to dry herself down.

'Your towel's really soft,' she sighed. 'Our one at home was really hard and scratchy and smelly cos Sean weed on it.'

'Oh dear,' I said. 'That can't have been very nice.'

I passed her the pyjamas that I'd dug out for her.

'They might be a little bit big because they're age nine but hopefully they'll do for tonight,' I said.

'I don't need no nappy neither,' she told me firmly. 'I don't do no wees and poos on the floor.'

'You're a big girl so I thought that might be the case.' I smiled at her. 'Don't worry, Sean and Dougie won't have to wear pull-ups forever. It's just until they get used to using the toilet. Did they do wees in the toilet at your house?'

Mary shook her head. 'They just did it on the floor or on the mattress in the night.'

'Well, it doesn't matter if they have an accident at night,' I reassured her. 'I can just put everything in the washing machine.'

'Our washing machine was broken,' she sighed sadly. 'And our cooker.'

'Oh dear,' I said. 'Your washing machine, your bath *and* your cooker were all broken. Did they used to work?'

'A long, long time ago,' she said wistfully.

Mary was a lot more verbal than her brothers and I sensed that through her I would be able to build up a picture of what their life at home had been like.

'Did you enjoy that bath?' I asked her as I helped her into the pyjamas.

She nodded.

'I smell funny though,' she said, sniffing her skin.

'That will be the soap.' I smiled. 'It smells like strawberries.'

It was sad that the feeling of being clean was so unfamiliar to her.

I could tell that Mary was lost in thoughts of her home, and a few minutes later she looked up at me, her blue eyes wide.

'Are we going back to our flat in a minute?'

'I don't think so, flower,' I told her gently. 'Your social worker will tell us more tomorrow but you're going to sleep here tonight. Is that OK?'

She nodded.

'Will I sleep with my brothers?' she asked, looking anxious.

'Would you like to sleep with them?' I replied. 'I've got enough rooms here that you can have your own bedroom or I've got one big bedroom with three beds in it.'

'No, I want to sleep with my brothers,' she said firmly.

Talking of her brothers, I realised I ought to go and check on the boys again. Things had been very quiet up until now but as we walked out of the bathroom, I saw Sean. He was at the top of the stairs balanced precariously on the top of the stairgate looking like he was about to leap down.

'Sean, no!' I shouted, my heart racing. 'You're going to fall. Get down from there right now.'

I ran round and pulled him off the top of the stairgate, then herded him and Mary back into the bedroom where Dougie was thankfully still glued to Peppa Pig. I was just starting to give Mary's hair another comb through when I heard a key in the front door. That would be Louisa.

Louisa was nearly twenty-one and she'd come to live with me when she was thirteen, following her parents' death in a car crash. She'd been with me for so long she was like my own daughter. Her boyfriend Charlie had recently proposed to her, and the two of them were saving up for their first flat. She worked as a nanny for a local family and was just returning from work.

'Maggie?' she yelled up the stairs a few minutes later. 'Are you there?'

The kids seemed calm for now so I ran out onto the landing to see her.

'Is everything OK?' she asked, a concerned look on her face. 'I just saw the kitchen and I wondered what on earth had happened.'

I realised I hadn't had time to clear it up since the children had ransacked it. There were toys all over the floor, the cushions had been pulled off the sofa and some of the cupboards emptied out. Not to mention the puddle of wee by the patio doors that I hadn't had a chance to mop up yet.

'A new placement arrived a little while ago so things have been a bit hectic,' I explained. 'Why don't you come up and meet them?'

'OK,' she said, looking intrigued.

As she walked upstairs, I had a quiet word with her.

'There are three of them,' I whispered. 'And just to warn you they're a little bit wild.'

'I can tell by the state of downstairs,' she replied. 'I thought we'd been burgled, Maggie.'

When Louisa walked into the bedroom, I introduced her to the children.

'This is my big girl, Louisa,' I told them 'She lives here too.'

'Louisa, this is Mary, Sean and Dougie. They've all been in the bath so they're nice and clean.'

The boys were totally oblivious and too engrossed in the DVD to respond, but Mary gave Louisa a shy smile.

'What lovely long hair you've got, Mary,' Louisa told her.

Mary blushed, looking pleased.

Bathtime might have been over but I knew at some point I had to get the children into bed. If bathtime was anything to go by, I knew I was in for another challenge. My mind was already on their bedroom. If these children were used to sleeping on the floor, it would be tricky to get one of them to settle in the top bunk. It would also be a safety risk, given how much leaping and climbing I'd witnessed already. Dismantling the bunk beds was going to be too big a job for Louisa and me to manage on our own, though.

'Louisa, would you mind sitting with the kids for a minute while I give Anne a ring?' I asked her, an idea coming to me.

The three of them were all now engrossed in Peppa Pig, and for the first time since they'd arrived, they were all quiet and calm. My friend Anne and her husband Bob lived a few minutes away and Bob had helped me put the bunk beds up in the first place. As he was a big, burly bloke, I knew he would be able to help dismantle them quickly.

Thankfully, Anne answered her mobile straight away.

'I'm ringing with a big favour to ask,' I told her.

I explained about the new placement and the issue I had with the bunk beds.

'Of course we can help,' she replied. 'Maggie, you sound frazzled.'

'I am a bit,' I laughed. 'I don't know whether I'm coming or going, to be honest.

'These kids have been through a lot and I'm just trying to help them feel as settled as they can after such a traumatic day.

'They've calmed down a bit since their bath but I'm not sure how long it's going to last.'

'Poor little loves,' sighed Anne. 'We're just finishing our tea but give us ten minutes and Bob and I will be round.'

'Thank you so much,' I said gratefully.

I also had another request before she hung up.

'I know this sounds odd, but please can you bring your old dog stairgate round too?' I asked.

'Of course I can,' she said. 'It's in the garage.'

As a single foster carer, I was really lucky to have such good friends close by who could help me out.

I'd already seen that Sean was daring enough to try and climb over the stairgate. A dog gate was taller and would hopefully be a lot harder for him to scale.

As promised, Anne and Bob arrived soon after and Bob got straight to work dismantling the bunk beds.

Half an hour later, there were three single beds in the room. Each one had clean bedding on already and a soft toy on each of the pillows, which was something I always liked to do when new children first arrived.

'Thank you so much,' I told him gratefully.

While he got on with fitting the dog gate at the top of the stairs, I knew I needed to try and get the boys to bed.

Louisa had dug out the basket of hair accessories and was showing Mary all the clips and bows. I felt a rush of gratitude. Louisa was invaluable in helping out with my placements, and I really didn't know what I was going to do without her when she moved out.

'Right, boys, it's time for bed now,' I told Sean and Dougie.

They looked at me, confused.

'No,' said Sean firmly. 'I ain't going to bed.'

'Food,' yelled Dougie. 'Want food.'

I knew that he wasn't going to be able to sleep if he was anxious about eating so I made both the boys a slice of toast each and a cup of warm milk so that their tummies wouldn't feel empty. Then I took them upstairs to the bathroom.

'We need to brush your teeth now,' I told them, showing them the Spiderman toothbrushes that I'd dug out of the cupboard. I could tell by the strange way they looked at the toothbrush as if it was some kind of alien object that brushing their teeth wasn't something they did on a day-to-day basis. They watched, puzzled, as I brushed my teeth.

'Your turn now,' I said cheerfully.

However, Dougie, eyeing the toothbrush with suspicion, refused point-blank to open his mouth. Sean looked puzzled and more out of curiosity, I think, held his mouth open for a couple of seconds before he clamped it firmly shut.

'No,' he yelled, pushing my hand away. 'Don't like it.'

They'd had a traumatic day and I didn't want to upset them any more before they went to sleep so I didn't push it.

I'll try again tomorrow, I told myself.

Now came the big challenge – getting them to bed. From everything I'd heard about their home life, it seemed unlikely that these children had ever had bedtimes or even their own beds, and had probably just fallen asleep wherever they were, at whatever time they wanted. All I could do was to start as I meant to go on by trying to get them into the security of a bedtime routine.

'It's night-night time now,' I told them. 'I'll show you where you're going to sleep.'

As soon as we walked into the bedroom, they started running around and leaping on the beds.

'Boys, it's time to get into bed now and get ready to sleep,' I told them gently but firmly.

The boys ignored me and kept tearing around the room. I managed to pick Dougie up, put him down on his bed and pull the duvet over him, and, much to my relief, he stayed put. Then I did the same with Sean.

There was a chair in the corner so I sat down on it and started reading them *The Three Little Pigs*.

Both boys stared at me in bemusement as if they couldn't understand what an earth I was doing. Dougie seemed to be enjoying it and snuggled down under the covers, his blue eyes wide as he lay there listening. Sean continued wriggling around, and after a few minutes he got up and started running around the room again.

'Back to bed,' I told him firmly, picking him up and putting him back into his bed.

I quickly finished the story and put the book down.

'It's night-night time now,' I told them softly, hoping that if I repeated it enough they'd eventually get the message.

I turned the main light off and left the lamp on. I went over to Dougie and tucked him in. The poor little lad looked up at me, terrified, as if it had just hit him that he was in a strange place.

'It's OK, sweetie, it's just sleepy time now,' I told him gently. 'Would you like me to sit on the chair over there until you fall asleep?'

He nodded, his big blue eyes filled with fear.

Sean was a different kettle of fish altogether. He refused to stay in his bed and was up and down like a yoyo.

'It's bedtime now, Sean,' I told him firmly. 'You need to stay in your bed.'

'No!' he shouted. 'I ain't tired. I wanna go downstairs.'

'No, Sean, it's night-time now. You can go downstairs tomorrow.'

I sat on the chair and mentally prepared myself for the fact that this was going to be a long night. Whatever happened, no matter how many times Sean got up, I stood my ground. I picked him up, put him back to bed and went and sat back on the chair.

'Lady, what you doing?' he called out to me. 'What you doing, lady?'

'I'm sitting here until you go to sleep like your brother,' I explained gently.

'Where's my sister?' he asked.

'She's downstairs,' I told him. 'And when you're asleep I'll bring her up and she'll go to sleep as well.'

'So she'll be here in the morning?'

'Yes, she'll be sleeping right next to you,' I promised.

But even that didn't reassure him and he refused to stay in bed. The next time I put him back I tried tucking the duvet in tightly at both sides and putting a blanket on top of him. Sometimes the extra weight can help make a child feel more secure, but even that didn't seem to have any effect.

Finally, nearly an hour and a half after I'd first taken them upstairs, Sean gave in. I saw his eyelids flutter and finally they closed.

I wearily trudged downstairs to find Anne and Louisa keeping Mary entertained with a jewellery-making kit. I knew the poor girl must be exhausted by now.

'Sorry I was so long,' I apologised to Mary. 'It took a while to get your brothers to sleep.'

Thankfully, Mary came upstairs quite easily, and I was struck again by how quiet and calm she was compared to her brothers.

24

When we got upstairs, she didn't run around like Sean and Dougie had, but my heart broke at the sight of her standing in her pyjamas looking so scared and alone, her eyes wide in her pale face.

'I'll leave the lamp on and there's a teddy there for you to cuddle,' I told her gently.

'OK.' She nodded.

She climbed into bed, the covers pulled up to her chin. She suddenly looked very young, and it was clear that she was terrified.

'Would you like me to sit on the chair until you fall asleep?' I asked her.

She shook her head firmly.

'OK, lovey. Well then, I'm going to go downstairs now but you just yell if you need me,' I said to her.

My heart went out to Mary. No matter how dirty their flat had been or how neglected and ignored these children had been by their parents, it was still home to them. To suddenly be taken away from everything that you'd ever known must be terrifying.

'Sleep well, Mary,' I whispered. 'Everything's going to be OK.'

By the time I came downstairs again I was utterly exhausted. Anne and Louisa were sitting at the kitchen table drinking too. Bob had already left.

'There's one there for you, Maggie,' Anne told me kindly. 'You look like you need it.'

As I sank down gratefully into the empty chair and picked up the warm mug, I realised that she and Louisa had tidied up the kitchen for me. Everything had been put back in its place and it was spotless.

'While you were sorting out the kids, I nipped to the super-market and got them all some pants and socks,' Anne told me. 'There are a variety of sizes there so hopefully they'll fit.'

I was so grateful, I could have cried.

'Oh, Anne,' I exclaimed. 'That's brilliant, thank you so much.'

'I knew you'd probably have spare clothes for them but it's nice for them to have their own underwear.' She smiled.

I sank back into my chair and had a long sip of tea.

'What a day,' I sighed. 'I didn't know when I got up this morning that I was going to have a new placement by the end of it.'

'I don't want to scare you but I think those three are going to be a challenge,' Louisa said, frowning a little.

'I think you're right.' I smiled. 'But you know me, I always like a challenge.'

After we'd said goodbye to Anne, I went up to check on the children. As I poked my head around the bedroom door I could see that Dougie was fast asleep in his bed, curled tightly around his teddy but my heart leapt when I saw that Sean and Mary's beds were empty. Then I spotted them. The two children were fast asleep on the floor, curled up together like little puppies. That was obviously how they were used to sleeping at home and they had craved that familiarity and comfort. My heart broke for these children whose normality involved sleeping on a hard floor and scavenging for whatever food they could. They'd only been here a few hours and I suspected that I'd only seen the tip of the iceberg regarding the neglect that they had suffered.

As gently as I could, I picked them both up and put them back into their beds. They looked peaceful now, so unlike the children who had rampaged through my house earlier. I knew their feral behaviour was a result of what they'd been through. If a child grows up without boundaries or discipline, how do they know how to behave? If no one shows a child love, care or attention, how can they feel secure or valued? They had been left to their own devices for the duration of their short lives and so they'd become like animals in order to survive – defecating on the floor, foraging for food and curling up and sleeping wherever they found themselves. I was determined to help these children but as I quietly tiptoed out of the room, I had no idea where to begin.

THREE

Wake-Up Call

It was the sound of a heavy object crashing to the floor that woke me. At first I thought I was dreaming but then I heard the banging and shouting coming from somewhere in the house and I realised that this was no dream. I sat up in bed and looked at the clock.

4.30 a.m.

Normally when a new placement arrives I find it difficult to settle but I must have fallen asleep as soon as my head hit the pillow. It still felt like the middle of the night but I could see that it was just starting to get light outside.

Thud. Smash.

My heart was pounding at the sound of the racket going on down the hallway. I quickly threw on my dressing gown and stumbled down the landing towards the children's room where the noise was coming from. My heart was in my throat as I tentatively pushed open the door, anxious at what I was about to see. The scene that greeted me could only be described as utter carnage.

Sean was standing on the chest of drawers and was trying to climb on top of the wardrobe. The curtains and curtain rail had been ripped down, the ceiling light was hanging by its wires as if someone had been swinging on it and the bedside table was on its side. All the books had been pulled out of the bookcase and the basket of toys had been emptied out all over the carpet. Dougie was naked and jumping from bed to bed like they were trampolines. He'd ripped his pull-up to shreds and much to my horror, there was poo smeared all over his legs, on the beds and up the walls. Unbelievably, Mary was still fast asleep despite the sound of the room being trashed around her. It gave me a stark insight into the noise level that she was used to sleeping through.

'What on earth is going on here?' I gasped, as the boys turned to look at me. 'Get down from there right now please, Sean.'

I lifted him off the chest of drawers.

'We don't climb on the furniture or swing on the lights, Sean. It's really dangerous,' I told him firmly.

The stench was unbearable and as I looked around the room I realised that there was poo everywhere. It was all over the radiator and even on the teddy bear that had been on Dougie's bed.

'Come on, Dougie, sweetie, let's go to the bathroom and get you cleaned up,' I told him gently. 'You come along too, Sean, so we don't wake your sister up.'

As horrified as I was, I knew there was no point in getting angry or telling them off. This was normal behaviour for them and neither of them knew any different. In the world they'd come from, furniture was for climbing on, things were there to be destroyed and you went to the toilet wherever you wanted to.

Poo smearing was about control. In Dougie's short little life, where and when he went to the toilet was the only thing that he had any say over. To him, it wasn't dirty or horrible, it was just how he'd lived. My house was clean and tidy and it didn't smell like home to him. No matter how awful his home life seemed to me, he was craving that familiarity because it was all that he had ever known.

It was too early in the morning to start running baths and I was keen to get the boys back to sleep as soon as possible, so I wiped Dougie down with baby wipes and put him in a new pull-up and some clean pyjamas.

'There, that should be more comfortable, lovey,' I told him gently. 'Next time you want to do a poo, it's much better to do it on the loo. We don't want to make your bottom any more sore.'

He glared at me angrily.

'No,' he hissed. 'Don't want to.'

He screwed up his face angrily and suddenly spat as hard as he could. Luckily this time it missed my face and landed on the floor.

'We don't spit in this house,' I told him. 'Spitting's not a nice thing to do, and it's yucky. Come on, let's wipe it up.'

I got a baby wipe and showed him how to clean it up off the floor.

'Please can you help me wipe it up, Dougie?'

'No!' he growled, giving me a kick.

'No kicking, please,' I said firmly, trying not to let the pain show on my face.

The boys needed to know that spitting and kicking wasn't acceptable behaviour, but I knew that getting angry with them wouldn't make any difference. All I could do was remain consistent in the way I dealt with it and hope that they'd eventually get the message.

I knew the other thing I needed to deal with as a matter of urgency was the poo situation in the bedroom.

'You two stay here and play with the bath toys while I go and sort your bedroom out,' I told them, desperately hoping that the toys would be enough to occupy them.

I'd been a foster carer for too many years to be squeamish about poo. I filled a bucket with hot water and bleach and grabbed some rubber gloves and a cloth. Mary was still sleeping soundly so I worked as quietly and quickly as I could. I stripped Dougie's bed and put the soiled sheets and his teddy into a bin bag. I washed down the walls and the radiator, trying my best not to gag at the smell.

Halfway through my clean-up, Mary stirred and opened her eyes.

'You go back to sleep, sweetheart, it's still very early,' I soothed.

As I wiped everything down I tried to work out what needed to be taken out of the room to make sure the boys couldn't do any more damage. I could take down the rail and curtains and just leave the blackout blind and swap the lampshade for one that was flat to the ceiling so it couldn't be swung on. There were a couple of pictures on the wall that I could swap for posters and I made my mind up to try and persuade Mary to move into her own room the following night.

There was nothing I could do about the curtains and the light right now, but I quickly took out the lamps and the bedside tables and put the books and toys into a pile on the landing. Then I remade Dougie's bed and went back into the bathroom.

'Back into your beds, boys,' I told them. 'It's not morning time yet. It's too early to get up now.'

I was amazed when both of them did as I'd asked and lay back down. I wasn't sure how long it was going to last but I wanted them to at least try to get another few hours' sleep.

As I came out of the bedroom and onto the landing, I could still smell the soiled sheets even though they were in a bin bag. I knew I wouldn't be able to rest until they were in the washing machine.

I went downstairs and put them on a hot wash along with a huge scoop of disinfectant powder. It was just after 5 a.m. by now. Remarkably it was all quiet upstairs but I knew there was no way I was going to be able to get back to sleep now, so I made myself a cup of tea and sank down into a chair at the kitchen table. It was a sunny summer morning and I took a moment to savour the peace and stillness. I had a feeling that it wasn't going to last long.

I was right. Just after 6 a.m. I heard the boys banging about. I ran upstairs to get them before their sister woke up.

'Let's go and get some breakfast,' I told them, ushering them downstairs.

Even though they'd only just woken up, the boys were as wild as they had been earlier. Sean climbed onto the banister and started sliding down it while Dougie leapt down the steps two at a time. I lifted Sean off the banisters and steered them both into the kitchen.

As soon as I put Sean down, the two boys started hitting each other, chasing each other around as they ran back and forth along the hallway screeching.

'Back in here please,' I told them firmly, herding them both into the kitchen.

I was keen to make sure they didn't wake up Louisa or Mary. My kitchen door had a lock on the inside, which I bolted shut so they couldn't get out.

Normally when I gave children breakfast I'd put the boxes of cereal on the table so they could choose which one they wanted. I'd also do a pile of toast and put out jam, marmalade, Marmite and honey. However, after the way the kids had reacted the previous day, I knew that wasn't going to be a good option.

My first challenge was getting them to sit at the table. Yesterday Sean had scurried off into a corner and Dougie had eaten his tea sat on the floor underneath the table. I wanted to teach them that the kitchen was where we went to eat and that whenever we had a meal, we sat at the table.

The boys were currently wrestling each other on the floor.

'If you'd like some breakfast, then I need you to sit down at the table please,' I told them.

They ignored me and kept on rolling around, giggling and squealing.

'Boys, I can't do breakfast until you're sitting down on your seats at the table,' I repeated, trying to make myself heard over the noise.

Again they didn't listen. I walked calmly over to Dougie, picked him up, carried him over to the table and put him down on a chair. He looked up at me, surprised.

'It's breakfast time, sweetheart, and you need to sit at the table,' I told him gently. 'Are you coming, Sean, or do I need to carry you too?'

'No,' he spat. 'Not coming.'

I walked over to him, picked him up and carried him over to the table too. He kicked and struggled in my arms but I managed to contain him.

'Now you're both sitting down, I can make breakfast.' I smiled.

They both looked a bit bemused. It was only their first day with me but my philosophy as a foster carer has always been that the minute a child steps through your front door, you ensure that every single rule stays in place. It doesn't matter how badly they've been neglected or what they've been through before arriving in your home. Children needed to know that in my house, I had certain rules that I expected them to follow, and that I was the one in charge. It's much harder to suddenly add rules weeks or months down the line. Children who are in the care system need this consistency. They need boundaries and routine, even if it isn't something they've ever had before. Rules and structure let them know where they stand and help them to feel secure and safe enough to be able to attach to you. It was especially important for children like Sean, Dougie and Mary who'd had no boundaries whatsoever and had been left to do whatever they liked.

My struggle at getting the boys to sit still was far from over, though. Over the next twenty minutes we had a battle of wills as the boys got up from the table over and over again and went running off. They seemed to think it was a game. Every time they climbed down, I calmly picked them up and carried them back until finally they got the message. Once they stayed sitting down I got some bowls out and put them on the table.

'If you're still sitting on your bottoms, then I'll get the spoons out,' I added.

They watched me like a pair of hawks and as soon as I put a Weetabix in each of their bowls, they tucked in hungrily. It was gone in seconds. I offered them another one and they wolfed that down in record speed too.

'Shall I make some toast?' I asked them and they both nodded, their eyes wide.

While I was sorting out some jam, Sean got up from the table and started climbing on top of the toy cupboard.

'Sean, have you finished breakfast?' I asked him.

He shook his head.

'Well I'm afraid there won't be any toast unless you're sitting down,' I told him.

He soon got the message when he saw Dougie tucking in and came running back to the table.

'More, more,' chanted Dougie after he'd finished.

I made them one more slice each and gave them a drink of milk.

'More, more,' Dougie begged again.

I knew after two Weetabix and two slices of toast that they were likely to be full, and I shook my head.

'No, there's no more now, sweetheart,' I told him. 'Breakfast is over but you can have a snack later.'

'No!' he shouted. 'Want more now.'

As I reached over to take away his empty plate, he sunk his teeth into my arm.

'No biting, Dougie,' I told him firmly. 'I won't have biting in this house.'

I knew they were eating not because they were hungry but because they were scared there wasn't going to be any more food. They didn't have any understanding of what it felt like to be full.

I knew from past experience that this was going to take them weeks or even months to get over. You could constantly reassure children that there was always going to be food, take them shopping and show them full cupboards, but sadly it took a long time for fears like that to fade and for children to believe that they were not going to go hungry.

Just then there was a quiet tapping on the kitchen door. I unlocked it to find Mary standing there in her pyjamas looking nervous.

'Hello, lovey.' I smiled at her. 'Did you have a good sleep? Would you like some breakfast?'

She nodded and, after gently reminding her a couple of times, she seemed to understand that she needed to sit at the table. As she was eating her cereal and toast, Dougie suddenly ran over and tried to snatch the toast from her hands.

'F**k off you little b****rd!' she shouted at him. 'That's mine!'

I was stunned. Although I'd heard much worse during my time as a foster carer, Mary seemed such a meek little thing, and I certainly hadn't been expecting that sort of language.

'Mary, I can see that you're cross but it would be great if you could use some different words,' I suggested.

She shrugged and carried on eating. Dougie wasn't going to give up without a fight and he lunged for her plate again.

'No, Dougie,' I told him, firmly lifting him away. 'You've had your breakfast.'

It was important for Mary to know that the food was hers and she was free to eat her breakfast in peace. I picked him up and carried him away but he struggled to free himself.

I eventually managed to distract him with the contents of the toy cupboard that Sean had already started pulling out.

Earlier that morning, before they'd woken up, I'd done a quick sweep of the kitchen and removed anything that might get easily damaged, lost or broken. I'd taken away all of the Lego and most of the board games. I'd put all my favourite china high up on the dresser and removed a vase of flowers that my boyfriend Graham had brought me from the kitchen table and put it on a shelf. I knew I'd done the right thing because before long the entire contents of the toy cupboard were scattered all over the floor.

Louisa's face fell when she came down for breakfast.

'They like making a mess, don't they?' she sighed, giving me a weak smile. 'Well, at least they slept OK.'

'So you didn't hear the 4.30 a.m. wake-up call?' I laughed.

She looked shocked when I told her what had happened.

'I'm really sorry, Maggie,' she said. 'You should have woken me and I could have given you a hand.'

'Don't be daft, lovey.' I grinned. 'After all these years of fostering, you know I'm not fazed by a bit of poo and a trashed bedroom.'

Sometimes I had to make a joke of things otherwise I'd cry.

'Do you think they need any medication?' she asked quietly, watching Dougie and Sean wrestle each other. 'You know, do you think they've got ADHD or something?'

I knew Louisa was familiar with this sort of thing as I'd fostered many children over the years with additional issues like autism and Asperger's.

'It's probably too early to say but my instincts are telling me probably not,' I told her. 'I think it's just down to the fact that they've had a life without boundaries. They've been left to run wild.'

Talking of which, I knew I needed to sort out their bedroom, which would be a lot easier without them around.

'Before you go to work, would you mind keeping an eye on them for ten minutes while I quickly do a few things upstairs?' I asked Louisa.

'No, of course not,' she said.

'Make sure you lock the door behind me so you can keep them in here,' I warned her.

I quickly bustled around the bedroom removing anything that could be a hazard. I took down the curtain pole and curtains leaving the blackout blind underneath, then I took down the pictures on the wall and unscrewed the lampshade from the ceiling. I was hoping Bob might be able to pop round later and put up another light fitting for me. Then I sorted out some clothes for them to get dressed in for the day and remembered the pants and socks Anne had bought them the day before. As I put my hand into the drawer I grimaced when I realised that all the underwear was sopping wet. My heart sank as the strong stench of ammonia filled my nostrils.

Someone had weed in the chest of drawers.

I felt like crying. Throwing everything into the washing basket for the second time that morning, I filled a bucket with hot water and bleach again. I knew that toilet-training was something that I needed to tackle straight away.

Toilet-training a five- and seven-year-old is no different to training a toddler. It was all about routine. As soon as Louisa had left for work, I took Dougie to the downstairs loo.

'See if you can see do a wee for me, sweetie,' I said, sitting him on the toilet.

He looked completely confused and nothing happened but at least he sat there. Sean came along too and watched curiously.

'Now it's your turn, Sean,' I told him. 'You're a big boy so I'm sure you can sit on the toilet yourself.'

'No,' he grunted and ran off.

I didn't force the issue. Instead I set the alarm on my phone and ten minutes later when it went off, I took them to the toilet again. Dougie sat there and this time he managed a wee.

'Well done, Dougie!' I smiled, clapping my hands. 'You've done a wee. That's absolutely brilliant. When you've washed your hands let's go into the kitchen and I'll get you a biscuit.'

At the mention of a biscuit, Sean was suddenly very keen to try and do one too, but when he pulled down his pull-ups I saw that he'd soiled himself.

'Never mind,' I said brightly. 'I'll just nip upstairs and get you a clean pull-up and some trousers.'

At least it was in his pull-up and not on the floor, I told myself as I rushed upstairs. I grabbed some nappy bags and baby wipes out of the bathroom cupboard and realised that I'd used the last pull-up. I knew there was another box in the high cupboard in my bedroom. After finding a stool to stand on, I finally managed to get them down and pulled one out.

'Sorry it took me so long,' I said as I walked into the kitchen. I stopped dead in my tracks at the scene that awaited me.

The fridge door was wide open and what looked like the entire contents were scattered all over the kitchen floor. The children were crouched there gorging themselves on whatever they could find. Mary was drinking cold pasta sauce straight from the jar, Sean was biting the corner off a huge chunk of cheese and Dougie had tipped out a yogurt and was licking it off the floor.

An important part of fostering is looking like you're calm and in control even if inside you feel like screaming. I took a deep breath to compose myself.

'Oh dear, this looks like a bit of a mess,' I said calmly. 'If you're hungry, go and sit down at the table and I'll bring you all a snack.

'Dougie, if you want a yogurt, I'll get you one and you can eat it with a spoon,' I told him. 'Sean, if you want some cheese, I'll cut you a slice off and you can have it with a cracker.

'Mary, pasta sauce is much nicer hot than cold so how about we have that for tea tonight?'

Clutching their food tightly, the children did as I asked.

I wasn't angry with them; I just felt desperately sad knowing that they were so scared and fearful of going hungry. All I could do was keep reassuring them, give them consistency and routine and also, I reminded myself, buy a bloomin' big padlock for the fridge.

FOUR

First Days

Once I'd cleaned up the kitchen floor and put what I could back in the fridge, my next challenge was to try and get the children dressed. Their social worker Lisa had phoned to say she was coming round in half an hour to see how they were getting on and I didn't want them to still be in their pyjamas when she arrived. But as soon as I took them upstairs, Sean and Dougie started tearing around and clambering on the furniture. I ignored them for a minute and turned to Mary instead.

'Can you get yourself dressed, sweetie, or do you need me to help you?' I asked her.

I'd already laid out all of their clothes on the bed.

'I can do it,' she said confidently.

Dougie and Sean were a different matter, however.

'Boys,' I said in my most authoritative voice. 'It's time to get dressed.'

They both ignored me. Dougie was jumping on the bed and Sean was trying to climb on top of the wardrobe again.

'Sean, get down from there please, it's dangerous. Come and get your clothes on,' I told him firmly.

'F**k off,' he spat. 'Don't want to.'

Dougie giggled and tried to clamber onto the chest of drawers.

'Give 'em a good kicking, Maggie,' Mary told me matter-of-factly. 'It's the only way to make them behave.'

My face fell and I couldn't hide my shock.

'We don't hit each other in this house, sweetie,' I told her, composing myself quickly. 'We use our words instead.'

But clearly my words were having no effect whatsoever on these two boys. Eventually I managed to grab Dougie and lift him off the chest of drawers. He thrashed around in my arms, squealing and kicking.

'Time to get dressed now,' I grimaced, struggling to contain him.

'No,' he screamed at the top of his lungs. 'Don't want to.'

He kicked and punched and lashed out at me and I realised it was pointless. He was flailing around too much for me to get the shorts and t-shirt anywhere near him.

I loosened my grip and he wriggled out of my arms and onto the floor where he lay, crying and screaming and kicking the wardrobe in anger. Meanwhile Sean had jumped off the wardrobe and was now leaping from bed to bed.

'Your turn to get dressed, Sean,' I told him.

'No,' he said defiantly.

'Sean, you need to come here please so I can help you get dressed.'

'Don't want to,' he said, and began hurling himself against the bedroom wall.

'Please stop that, Sean, or you're going to hurt yourself,' I urged him.

I had two children who were totally out of control. One was lying on the floor having a meltdown while the other was literally bouncing off the walls. Mary, bless her, was dressed and ready, but I knew neither of the boys would listen to me in this state.

So I turned to a technique that a lot of people might find controversial. I quickly ran downstairs to the kitchen and got three ice pops out of the freezer. Then I bolted back upstairs.

'Well done for getting dressed,' I told Mary, handing her an ice pop. 'You sit down and eat that.'

I went over to Dougie who was still having a tantrum on the floor and held out an ice pop to him.

'Here you go,' I said cheerfully.

He stopped kicking and screaming and looked up at me, a puzzled look on his face.

'Go on,' I told him. 'Take it.'

He took it off me and sat there on the floor, giving it a good suck.

Sean looked equally as confused as I offered him an ice pop. He stopped throwing himself against the wall and snatched it from me.

Most people would probably question my sanity giving two children who were already out of control a sugary ice pop, but it's a very effective technique for children who are having a meltdown. It's something I don't use very often, but it's useful to call on in certain situations when things get desperate. The sucking action calms them down – just like a dummy soothes a baby. It helps lower their heart rate and blood pressure, reduces their stress levels and relaxes them.

Sometimes I use a lollipop instead but I prefer ice pops or ice lollies as the cold helps to regulate them.

Considering what these children had been through, a little bit of sugar wasn't going to kill them. I wasn't rewarding their behaviour, I was helping them to calm down before they hurt themselves. Children who have been through trauma often struggle to access the area of the brain that helps them calm themselves down, but giving them a lolly or an ice pop or even a bowl of ice cream can help them to do this.

It certainly worked on the boys. As Dougie sat on the floor calmly sucking on his ice pop, I was able to pick him up, put him on my knee and pull on a t-shirt and shorts. Sean had climbed down onto the bed to eat his and he was calm and compliant so I was able to do the same with him. Once I'd got them all dressed, I quickly made their beds and folded up their pyjamas, relishing the five minutes of calm as they happily tucked into their ice pops.

''Nother one?' asked Dougie hopefully, giving a satisfying smack of his lips as he finished his.

'No, lovey, they're all gone now.' I smiled. 'Let's go downstairs as Lisa will be here soon.'

Thankfully they were still quite calm when the doorbell rang five minutes later. Lisa had obviously learnt her lesson and was a lot more practically dressed today in black trousers and flat shoes.

'Hi, Maggie.' She smiled. 'I thought I'd pop round and see how you were all getting on.

'Hello, children,' she called to them.

They looked up at her but none of them said anything.

'I'll put the kettle on and see if they want to go out into the garden while we have a chat,' I told her.

The sun was still shining and I knew the garden was safe because it was enclosed and the gate at the bottom was locked. There was a climbing frame and a sandpit to keep them busy and when I opened the patio doors, all three of them couldn't wait to go out.

'So, Maggie, how's it been?' Lisa asked, as we watched them chase each other round through the kitchen window.

'To be honest, exhausting,' I sighed. 'They were up very early this morning and they'd trashed their bedroom. We've had poo smearing and lots of anxiety issues around food.'

'It's very early days and it's to be expected,' said Lisa with a sympathetic tilt of her head.

'Oh, I know.' I nodded. 'The boys are like two wild animals. As you saw last night, there's been a lot of spitting, kicking and swearing and they're never still. Thankfully Mary is much calmer and a lot more verbal than the two boys.'

I looked out at them playing. Mary was sitting on a swing and the two boys were wrestling each other on the grass.

'I'm having to be incredibly rigid with my rules around making them sit at the table to eat and trying to get them to learn to use the toilet.'

'It's hard but that's the right thing to do,' she reassured me. 'As we both know, what they need most right now is routine and structure.'

Lisa updated me about what was happening with the children's parents Kathleen and Darren. They'd been charged and were likely to be kept on remand.

'Given the severity of the charges it's likely that they're both going to go to prison,' she said. 'At this stage they're saying they're willing to give their permission for the children to stay in care.'

'Do they want to see the kids?' I asked.

Even parents who are in prison or on remand still have a right to see their children and I'd taken several children into prison for contact visits in the past.

Lisa shook her head.

'Unfortunately neither of them have shown any interest whatsoever, so with that in mind, Social Services are more than likely going to go for a full care order.'

'But it's such early days,' I sighed. 'They might change their minds.'

'That's true.' Lisa nodded. 'I'll give it a week or so and then go back to them to see if they'd like to have contact. But in all likelihood, Maggie, all the signs suggest that Social Services will go for a full care order.'

I always feel desperately sad for children when their parents don't want to see them. Even one brief contact visit to say goodbye can help children get some sort of closure that in the long term enables them to move on a lot quicker.

'Have the children been asking about their parents?' asked Lisa.

'The boys haven't said a word.' I shrugged. 'They've never even mentioned home.'

The only child who had shown a slight interest was Mary.

'Mary asked last night whether she was going home but I think that was more from confusion than anything else,' I said.

I knew that this meant that the children were likely to be with me for at least the next few weeks while Social Services came up with a long-term plan for their future.

'Maggie, are you OK to have them until we see how the land lies?' Lisa asked nervously.

'Yes, of course.' I nodded.

Although the past twenty-four hours had been exhausting, I desperately wanted to help these three little ones and give them a home where they felt safe and looked after. What they needed most at this moment was stability and security and I couldn't give up on them now and move them on. It would have gone against everything I believed in.

'Obviously we'll need to sort them out a school place as soon as possible,' Lisa said as she flicked through some paperwork.

'School?' I gasped, stunned. 'There's absolutely no way they could cope with starting school at this point in time. Definitely not the boys, anyway.'

'They'll have to,' replied Lisa. 'Social Services has a legal requirement to make sure kids their age are in full-time education.'

I shook my head.

'It's too soon,' I sighed. 'They're not even toilet-trained.'

How could I send a seven-year-old to school in pull-ups? They weren't able to sit at a table to eat, never mind sit still for hours in a classroom.

'They'd create havoc,' I told her. 'They'd trash the place.'

'The most I can give you is a couple of weeks' grace for them to settle in, but after that they must be in school,' Lisa said firmly, closing her notebook as if to say that was the end of discussion.

'Now, I suppose I'd better talk to the children about what's happening and let them know that they're staying with you for the foreseeable future,' said Lisa, suddenly looking nervous.

'I'll call them in for a snack and then you can chat to them,' I replied.

At the mention of food, all three of them came running inside in record speed.

'Would you like a biscuit?' I asked them and they all nodded eagerly.

'Come and sit down at the table with Lisa then.'

Mary did as I'd asked, but the boys started running around doing laps of the room. I made Lisa another cup of tea and got Mary a biscuit and completely ignored the two boys. Once they saw Mary tucking into a biscuit though, they quickly got the message and both came to sit down.

'Would you like a biscuit now?' I asked and they nodded.

Once they'd finished and had a drink of water, Lisa turned to them and cleared her throat, but Dougie and Sean had already slunk off their chairs and were crawling around the floor under the table.

'Boys, come and sit back down please,' she told them, a hint of desperation in her voice. 'I'd like to have a chat with you.'

However, they completely ignored her and ran back outside.

'Why don't you talk to Mary and I'll try and explain things to them later?' I suggested.

I knew it was going to cause more upset trying to get them to sit still and listen. Lisa nodded and turned to Mary.

'I wanted to let you know that your mummy and daddy are OK,' she told her gently. 'People are looking after them. But for the moment they'd like you to stay here with Maggie for a little while. Is that OK?'

Mary stared blankly at Lisa, her big blue eyes devoid of any emotion.

'Do you understand what I'm saying?' Lisa asked her. 'You and your brothers are going to stay with Maggie for the time being. Is there anything you'd like to ask me?'

Mary paused and looked thoughtful for a minute.

'Last night Maggie washed my hair and her big girl Louisa put some bows and clips in it,' she said.

Lisa looked a bit bemused.

'You're right.' I smiled. 'Louisa did do your hair last night but we can talk about that later. At the moment Lisa's trying to tell you something very important about your mummy and daddy. Did you hear what she said?'

Mary turned away and gazed out of the window.

'My hair looked really pretty with them bows and clips in, didn't it?' she sighed, refusing point-blank to engage in any conversation about her parents.

When children are uncomfortable with what someone is saying, they will often try to create a distraction or change the subject and talk about something completely irrelevant.

'OK, Mary, you can go outside with your brothers if you want,' Lisa told her, giving up.

But she stayed in the kitchen to play. Lisa and I gave each other a look to indicate we'd talk about it later.

Lisa glanced out of the patio doors to the garden and almost spat out her tea.

'What on earth are those boys doing out there?' she gasped.

Mary ran to the door and I looked out to see Sean lying on the grass face up and Dougie face down, writhing around on top of him. To my shock and dismay, I could hear the loud moans and groans they were making through the open doors.

'Oh they're just sexing.' Mary smiled matter-of-factly. 'They're pretending to sex each other, that's all.'

A look of pure horror flashed across Lisa's face.

I ran out into the garden where Sean and Dougie were still gyrating on top of each other.

'Let's not do that, thank you,' I instructed firmly, lifting Dougie off his brother. 'How about you go and play in the sandpit before we say bye bye to Lisa.'

Mary ran out to join them and thankfully they were quickly distracted by some plastic diggers.

Lisa looked horrified.

'What on earth must they have seen at home?' she sighed, shaking her head.

'Far too much by the look of it,' I replied.

'Do you think there's the possibility they've been abused?' she asked.

'It's something we definitely need to keep a close eye on,' I told her. 'Hopefully they're displaying sexualised behaviour because of what they've observed rather than having been subjected to it themselves.'

Sadly some neglected children showed sexualised behaviour after seeing their parents or other adults have sex in front of them. It was a really difficult area as we didn't know if it was something they'd accidentally witnessed or it was something they'd been deliberately exposed to. If it was deliberate, it would be classed as child abuse but that was very difficult to prove. They could even have been copying something that they'd seen in a film or a TV programme. There was no doubt it was shocking to see five- and seven-year-olds simulating sex with each other, but knowing the dysfunctional household the children had come from, with people taking drugs and coming and going at all hours, in a way, it wasn't surprising.

'All the children had a full medical before I brought them to you and there was no physical evidence of abuse but just be vigilant,' Lisa told me. 'If they're showing any other signs of possible sexual abuse, then we need to alert the police.'

'I'll keep a close eye on things,' I promised.

Lisa finished her tea and the children eventually came running back in.

As Lisa was talking to me about filling in some forms, Dougie wandered over to her and climbed onto her lap.

'Oh, hello there, little man,' she said, looking slightly uncomfortable that this grubby child was clambering all over her. We carried on chatting but after a minute, I noticed Dougie had started doing what I could only describe as humping her leg.

'Look he's sexing you now, Lisa,' screeched Mary. 'He likes you. Are you gonna show him your boobs?'

'Yeah, show him your boobs,' yelled Sean.

'Boobies, boobies, boobies,' he chanted.

Lisa looked mortified and was very flustered. I jumped up and lifted Dougie off her leg.

'No thank you, Dougie,' I told him firmly. 'It's not nice to do that to Lisa's leg. How about you go back and play in the garden?' I suggested. 'You could make some sandcastles in the sandpit.'

I knew from experience the best way to handle behaviour like that was to quickly and calmly put a stop to it and then distract them. If you made a fuss about it or got angry, the child might repeat the behaviour in the future in order to get attention or provoke a reaction.

I could tell that Lisa couldn't get away from the house fast enough. She stood up and grabbed her bag.

'Well unfortunately I've got to go now, but I'll be back to see you in a day or so,' she told the children. 'Maggie, I'll be in touch.'

'OK.' I nodded.

Then she hurried out of the door without a backwards glance.

Over the next couple of days I kept things very quiet and low-key. We didn't see anyone or go out anywhere in a bid to help the children feel more settled and make some progress with toilet-training. I stuck to a rigid routine for meal times and bed times in the hope that it would calm them down. I also managed to persuade Mary to move into the other bedroom.

'But what about Dougie and Sean?' she asked, looking concerned. 'They won't be able to sleep without me there.'

'They'll be fine,' I reassured her. 'This way if they get up early, they won't wake you up and I'm just down the landing.'

I was more worried that Mary herself wouldn't be able to get to sleep without her brothers as she wasn't used to being alone. But thankfully, from the first night, she was fine and I think she enjoyed the fact that she had her own space away from her boisterous brothers.

The boys were still creating chaos and any room would be trashed within seconds of them entering it. I'd become a master of staying calm and not reacting. I needed to give the impression that I was completely in charge and nothing fazed me, even in the moments when I was raging inside.

Everything was still a battle, from getting dressed in the morning to getting them to sit at the table to eat to putting them to bed at night, but I was determined to stick it out. I knew it wasn't their fault. They'd never had any kind of routine before, they were in a strange house and this was all new to them.

I was determined to crack meal times and get the boys to sit at the table while they ate and not run off.

'Why don't you get those Ikea chairs out?' suggested Louisa when she came home one night after work. 'You know, those two in the garage.'

'You're a genius!' I exclaimed.

I'd completely forgotten about the two little wooden chairs. They had long legs like highchairs and rounded arms on them so if the boys were sitting on them and they were pushed into the table they couldn't wiggle out. As well as encouraging them to sit at the table, I also needed to show them how to use cutlery. I gave them very simple food at first – lots of finger foods on plates. I also gave them lots of yogurt or Angel Delight so they could practise using a spoon.

I also started enforcing some simple manners. I was a big believer in making sure all the children that I fostered were polite and said 'please' or 'thank you'. Manners cost nothing and people always notice a polite child.

'Would you like a piece of bread and butter?' I asked Sean one morning.

He grunted in reply.

'We say "yes please" in this house. Can you say "yes please", Sean?' I asked him. '"Please" is the magic word and I can't go and get you bread and butter until I hear it.'

'Yes please,' he sighed begrudgingly.

'Peas, peas, peas,' shouted Dougie, desperate to get his own slice.

Mary giggled.

'It's "please", Dougie, not "peas" you silly b****rd,' she told him.

I was still working on the bad language . . .

Despite my continual attempts to reassure them, all the children still had the overwhelming fear that they were going to go hungry. One night after Sean had finished off his sausage and mash, he reached over to my plate, stuck his fist into my mashed potato and scooped a big bit into his mouth.

'No, Sean,' I told him firmly, removing his hand from my plate. 'That's my dinner. If you're still hungry after everyone has finished, then I'll get you something else.'

The other two children were the same. They'd grab hand-fuls of peas from Louisa's plate or a fistful of pasta off mine.

Toilet-training was also proving to be a hard slog. As is often the way, little ones tend to get the hang of it more quickly so Dougie was making more progress than Sean. I was still setting my alarm and encouraging them to sit on the toilet several times an hour and they got a Smartie every time they tried.

After several more poo-smearing incidents, I'd started putting Dougie in a nappy and a onesie at night and I'd put both of them on him backwards so it was much harder for him to take them off.

In those early days I clung to the small victories. Bedtimes were slowly getting shorter as they got used to getting into bed and they all seemed to love me reading them stories. Even though it was hard, the only thing I could do was be rigid and consistent and hope that in the end, it would work and these children would start to respond.

FIVE

Supermarket Shame

After three days in the house, I decided it was time to bite the bullet and venture out in public with the children. Because of all their anxiety around food and eating, I wanted to take them to the supermarket. I hoped that seeing me buy a trolley full of shopping would help it sink in that food was readily available at my house and remove some of their fear about being hungry. It would also be a chance to get them some much-needed clothes and let the boys choose some pants to help encourage their toilet-training.

They were sitting eating breakfast when I explained my plan.

'This morning we're going to go out to the supermarket,' I told them in an excited voice. 'We're going to buy some food and you all need some new clothes. So after breakfast we're going to put our shoes on and get in the car.'

The boys didn't show any reaction but Mary shook her head.

'They're not gonna like that, Maggie,' she sighed. 'They don't like cars.'

'I'm sure they'll like it in my car.' I smiled at her optimistically.

After breakfast and the long, painful process of trying to get them to brush their teeth, it was time to get them in the car. I had a black people carrier that had room for three car seats in the first row. Mary and Sean were tall enough to sit in a high-backed booster that just used the normal seat belt. However, as Dougie was small, he would go into a car seat with a five-point harness. I lifted him in first.

'No, don't like it!' he yelled, arching his back in protest so it made it impossible for me to fasten the buckle.

'You can choose some big boy pants at the shop,' I told him, desperately trying to distract him while I fed his arms through the straps and tried to force the buckle closed. 'Do you want Paw Patrol or Octonauts? Or what about Spiderman?'

'No,' he yelled, straining. 'Out! Out!'

There was no placating him. He screamed and cried and wriggled but I persevered and eventually I heard the satisfying click of the buckle.

I took a deep breath. One down, two to go.

Mary, bless her, climbed in without any argument and sat down obediently while I fastened the seat belt for her. Sean, however, was a different kettle of fish.

'Let's strap you in now, Sean.' I smiled, pulling the seat belt across his front and clicking it in place.

A couple of seconds later, he pressed the red tab and clicked it off again.

'No, Sean,' said Mary anxiously. 'You've got to leave it.'

'Don't want to,' he yelled.

Next to him Dougie was still shouting and thrashing around.

This is going to be an interesting journey, I thought to myself.

'Sean, you need to keep your seat belt on,' I told him firmly, clicking it back into place.

'Right,' I said, sitting back in the driver's seat and wiping the beads of sweat from my brow. 'Off we go.'

Within thirty seconds of setting off down the road, I heard a familiar click.

'Maggie, he's taken it off again,' yelled Mary.

I immediately pulled over.

'Sean, I can't drive unless you stay in your seat belt,' I explained. 'It's too dangerous.'

'No,' he shouted. 'Don't want to.'

'I'm afraid you have to,' I said, clicking it back into place.

'Out, out!' yelled Dougie.

I set off again but a few minutes later he'd done it again. After the fourth time, we hadn't travelled more than a mile and I'd had enough. This time I pulled up, rummaged in the boot and found some additional straps for the car seat, then I climbed in the back. I lifted him out of his seat and onto Mary's knee.

'You sit with Mary a minute,' I told him.

As I attached the new straps to the car seat, I chatted to the children.

'Look out of the window and tell me who can see a blue car,' I said.

'Me!' yelled Dougie.

'Now can you spot a red one?' I asked.

It was annoyingly fiddly but finally I'd managed to attach the new five-point harness that would hopefully be trickier for Sean to get out of.

'Right, come and sit back in your seat now, Sean,' I said. 'Different straps this time.'

He was so busy looking out the window for a red car that thankfully he didn't seem to notice as I strapped him in the new harness.

Before he could say anything I'd got back in the front and started up the engine. I glanced in my mirror and could see Sean fiddling with the new straps and then getting angry when he realised he couldn't just click it open like the other one.

'Get it off,' he shouted. 'I want it off.'

As soon as the engine started, Dougie began yelling again too.

'Go back,' he screamed. 'Go back.'

Amid all this chaos, Mary was quiet in the back.

'Are you OK, Mary?' I called to her above the din.

I glanced in the rearview mirror and saw the anxious look on her face.

'We went this way before,' she murmured, staring out of the window.

'When was that?' I asked gently.

'When we was with that lady,' she explained. 'The one that took us to you. Are we going home, Maggie?' she asked, her blue eyes wide with fear. 'Is that where you're taking us?'

The poor girl looked absolutely terrified.

'No, sweetie,' I soothed. 'Remember how Lisa explained that you're going to be staying with me for a little while? I'm taking you to the supermarket and you and the boys are going to help me choose some food and we'll get you some new clothes. Then afterwards we'll go back to my house again.'

She nodded but I could see the anxiety etched into her face.

To be honest, I wasn't surprised at the way the children had reacted. Car journeys are often traumatic for children who've been taken into care. They associate being removed from their birth family with a car journey accompanied by a social worker who's a complete stranger, and their brain stores this information as a traumatic event. Children get scared about where you're taking them or they worry that they might be moving to another place. Putting them in car seat can also make them feel trapped and out of control and their fight or flight mechanism is triggered. I knew the boys were also frustrated because they didn't have my attention while I was driving. Their usual behaviour might get negative attention but at least it was something. When I was driving I had my back to them, which they might have perceived as rejection or being forgotten or ignored.

Although I knew their behaviour was understandable, it didn't make it any less stressful. Dougie and Sean were still crying, shouting and thrashing around in the back seat. I put on a CD of children's music to see if that would help calm and distract them but it didn't make one iota of difference.

The supermarket was only a ten-minute drive but by the time I pulled up into the car park, my head was ringing from all the noise and the boys looked exhausted.

'Out. Out now,' wailed Dougie desperately, his face and t-shirt saturated with tears.

'I promise that I'll get you out in a minute,' I soothed. 'Watch me walk over to get a trolley.'

I wheeled it over and lifted Dougie out of the car. I could feel his little body relax with relief in my arms.

'You're OK,' I told him. 'Look, we're at the shop now.'

I strapped him into the front seat of the trolley, then got Mary and Sean out of the car.

'You two can walk and I'd like you to hold onto the trolley,' I told them. 'Any messing about or running off, Sean, and I'll put you in the trolley with your brother.'

Thankfully as we walked into the supermarket, the boys were both quiet. They looked around in awe like they'd never seen anything like it before. They both seemed over-whelmed by the bright lights, the people and the tannoy announcements.

'Did you used to go shopping with Mummy and Daddy?' I asked Mary.

She shook her head.

'Not the boys and not with Mummy and Daddy. I went by myself sometimes. But my shop wasn't big like this.'

Amazingly they were all very quiet until we walked up the biscuit aisle.

'Want them!' Dougie shouted excitedly, pointing at a packet of Hobnobs.

I let them choose a packet each. However, Sean started running up and down grabbing packets of biscuits and throwing them into the trolley.

'Sean, please put them back,' I told him firmly. 'We've already got three packets of biscuits in the trolley so we don't need any more.'

'No,' he shouted, grabbing some digestives and Rich Tea.

'Put them back please, Sean,' I said firmly.

'No,' he yelled, kicking the trolley. 'F**k off.'

Other shoppers were starting to look over at the commotion and were giving me disapproving looks.

'Sean,' I said, trying to keep my voice down. 'Put the biscuits back on the shelf, otherwise I will.'

'You're a b***ch!' he yelled at the top of his voice.

'I might well be, but you're still not having any more biscuits,' I told him calmly, getting them out of the trolley and putting them back on the shelf.

I saw the shock on the faces of passers-by and I wanted the ground to swallow me up. Sean was in a proper rage by now. He was shouting and swearing and kicking the displays. I felt my face going bright red as a woman steered her daughter down another aisle to avoid us, and the rest of the shoppers gave us a wide berth.

The language coming out of Sean's mouth was terrible but as a rule I don't worry too much about swearing as I know it's learnt behaviour. I don't swear around children so I know that in time, it will change. But to other people overhearing Sean's meltdown, it looked like I was the world's worst mother.

'Tell me when you're ready to carry on,' I told Sean, keeping my voice neutral.

We stood there and waited while he kicked and screamed and threw himself around on the floor.

'We're just waiting for your brother to calm down, then we'll carry on with our shopping,' I explained to Mary and Dougie, who were looking bemused. 'Would you like a biscuit while we're waiting?'

I opened the packet of Hobnobs and handed them one each. I saw Sean watching me out of the corner of his eye. Suddenly the noise stopped and he sat up.

'Can I have one?' he asked.

'Well if you get up off the floor and hold onto the trolley until we get to the till, then you can have one while I pay for the shopping,' I said. 'But if there's any more shouting or messing about, then you won't get a biscuit.'

Sean quickly got up and wandered over to the trolley.

'Are you ready to carry on?' I asked him and he nodded sheepishly.

When children kick off in public like that, it can be mortifying but I refused to let it bother me too much. If people knew the real situation and what was going on behind the scenes, they probably wouldn't be so quick to judge.

Amazingly, the promise of a Hobnob was enough to enable Sean to calm down. A couple of times he let go of the trolley and started to wander off.

'I'm only doing biscuits for those whose hands stay on the trolley,' I warned loudly and he quickly came back again.

While my stand-off with Sean had been going on, I noticed that Mary had been walking quietly ahead.

'Are you OK, lovey?' I asked her.

'Hmm,' she mumbled.

But when she turned round, I noticed her hoodie looked strange and the front was all bulky. I didn't say anything to her but as we walked down the aisle, I saw her hand reach out for a packet of chewing gum and she quickly tucked it under her top.

She was shoplifting.

When we had everything we needed, I turned to her as we walked up to the till.

'Mary, have you got anything you want to put in the trolley before I pay?'

'No.' She shrugged.

'Are you sure?' I asked calmly. 'Your hoodie looks very heavy. Why don't you unzip your top and we can have a look at what you've got?'

Sheepishly Mary undid her hoodie to reveal some sweets and chewing gum, a packet of biscuits and some lip balm.

'Well we know we don't need biscuits because we've already got some in the trolley and I'm not buying sweets today. But the lip balm is a good idea. Next time, you can just say, Maggie I need some lip balm, and I'll put some in the trolley. Do you think you can do that, Mary?'

She nodded her head, not looking at me, her cheeks pink.

'Good.' I smiled. 'We don't need to put things down our jumpers when we go shopping otherwise the person on the till won't be able to see it.'

I hoped Mary had got the message.

'You get lots more things if you pay with money, don't you, Maggie?' she said as she helped me to load it all onto the conveyor belt.

'What do you mean?' I asked, confused.

'I can't get this much down my jumper when I nick stuff, can I?' She smiled.

I gave her a sympathetic smile.

'You're right.' I nodded. 'It's much better paying for things than nicking stuff.'

As difficult as it was, I knew she was only doing what she was used to. From everything I'd seen so far, it seemed likely that the children were only able to eat when they stole food. Their reaction to the supermarket was a good insight into what their life had been like before, although it was horrendously sad that this was normal behaviour to them.

As I finished paying for the shopping I let out a sigh of relief that our supermarket trip was almost over. Then I smelt an overwhelming stench.

'Poo,' squealed Mary. 'There's poo coming down Dougie's leg.'

With a feeling of dread, I looked down at Dougie. He looked sheepish and, sure enough, he had soiled himself and it had leaked out of the pull-up he was wearing.

'OK then, let's quickly go to the toilet,' I said.

I managed to get all three children plus the trolley full of shopping into the toilet while I sorted Dougie out. Thankfully I was able to put him in some new pants and shorts that I'd just bought.

By the time I'd wheeled everyone back to the car, I was utterly exhausted. I was dreading the drive home in case the boys kicked off again. However, there were a few little things I could try. I'd bought some snack boxes of raisins at the supermarket so I gave a box to each child, knowing that it would give them something else to focus on. I also had a couple of fleecy blankets in the boot. I rolled them up into sausage shapes and once the boys were strapped in, I placed them around their necks like travel pillows.

'This will make it all nice and comfy for you.' I smiled at Dougie.

It was a distraction but also it would help them feel secure in their car seats. If they felt really stressed, then they could wrap themselves in the blankets or even get under them.

I made a mental note to get them all to bring a teddy each from my house next time we were going in the car to give them something familiar to hold. In an ideal world, it would also have helped to have another adult who could sit in the back with them and reassure them.

I chatted and sang nursery rhymes all the way home and thankfully this time they were much calmer.

As I pulled into my street, I breathed a sigh of relief. It was only 11 a.m. but I felt as exhausted as I would have at the end of the day. The supermarket trip had been an ordeal for all of us but I knew that these were all new experiences for the children and it would take time for them to get used to all the changes.

I was just debating how to get the shopping and the children into the house and which way round to do it when I saw a familiar red car pull up.

The dark-haired driver smiled and I felt a wave of relief. It was my link worker Becky from the fostering agency that I worked for.

'You've arrived at the perfect time,' I sighed gratefully.

'You look shattered, Maggie,' she exclaimed. 'What's happened?'

'We've been to the supermarket and it's nearly killed me,' I laughed. 'Do you mind giving me a hand getting the shopping into the house while I get the kids in?'

I quickly introduced the kids to her and got them into the house. I opened the patio doors and they ran out into the garden.

'Gosh you've got your hands full there, Maggie,' she said as we hauled the bags inside. 'How are things going?'

'To be honest, it's been a bit of a nightmare but it's such early days,' I sighed.

'Feeding them is a nightmare, getting them dressed is a nightmare, going out is a nightmare. Two of them aren't toilet-trained and the social worker wants them to be in school in a week.'

Becky looked concerned at my outburst.

'Right, first of all we need to look into getting a respite carer,' she said, springing into action. 'That will give you some time to at least sort out the school places and take the children up individually to meet their teachers and see the classroom.

'It will be far too much trying to settle all three children in at once. You can't spread yourself too thinly and another new start will be overwhelming for them.'

I was glad Becky was here. She was always very good at thinking of practical solutions when I was panicking.

'I know in your notes that you emailed over you said that Mary was calmer and a lot more verbal than the boys so perhaps you could arrange it so she could start school first, giving you a bit more time to work with her brothers?' she suggested.

'Good idea,' I said.

'If I try and find a respite carer ASAP, then maybe Mary could even start this week.'

'That's so soon,' I sighed.

All of the children had been through so much upheaval.

'To be honest, Maggie, there's not much difference between starting this week and next. She might surprise you and enjoy it.'

Deep down, I knew I probably did need the help of a respite carer, but I was worried that introducing someone new and disrupting our routine would be too much for the siblings to cope with this early on.

I explained my concerns to Becky.

'I don't think I want them to go into another carer's home at this point. This morning on the way to the supermarket, Mary got worried that they were going back to their old house. I want them to feel safe and secure with me and know that they're not getting sent away.'

'Well, in that case, how about I try and find a carer who can come here to your house instead?' Becky suggested.

It had only been a matter of days since the children had arrived. I was trying my hardest to give them some stability, security and routine and it felt wrong fobbing them off on another carer so soon. But I knew my hands were tied. As a single carer, I didn't have anyone else who could take over from me and it wasn't fair to ask Louisa to take time off work. Normally my friend Vicky, a fellow foster carer, helped me out, but she was fostering three children at the moment and I knew it would be impossible for her to cope with these three as well.

When I went to bed that night my head was spinning. How on earth were these vulnerable, unruly kids going to manage with being left with another carer, not to mention the even bigger challenge of starting school for the first time? Were they going to be able to cope with everything we were about to throw at them or was it all going to come crashing down like a house of cards?

SIX

School Days

My heart sank as I saw the familiar number flash up on my phone.

'Graham,' I sighed apologetically, as I answered. 'I'm so sorry. You've been on my mind but I completely forgot to call you back the other day.'

'It's all right, Maggie, I'm not chasing you up,' he replied. 'I was just worried about you, that's all.'

Graham and I had been dating for the past couple of years or so. He was a physiotherapist in his early forties. He was everything that I looked for in a man – tall, salt and pepper hair, and he was a kind and gentle person. When we'd first got together I'd been very upfront and honest about my fostering and how it didn't give me much time for a social life. He was very understanding, but as the months had gone by, I sometimes sensed that he became exasperated when a new child came in and I'd completely disappear for a few weeks.

'I assumed you'd got a new placement in and that was taking up your time,' he told me.

'You know me too well,' I said. 'You're absolutely right. I've got three new children in and they're running me ragged.'

'Three?' he gasped. 'I'm not surprised.'

'Every night when the kids have gone to bed I've been going to ring you, but to be honest, bed times have been taking me so long that by the time I come downstairs I'm shattered,' I explained.

'I even typed out a text to you the other night but I must have forgotten to press Send.'

'Maggie, honestly don't worry,' he reassured me. 'I was ringing to check you were OK, not to tell you off.'

'I'll keep in touch and when things calm down a bit we can meet up,' I promised. 'The kids are due to start school soon and once they're settled in, I'll be free during the day.'

'It sounds like you've got your work cut out,' he sympathised.

The second I put the phone down to Graham, my mobile rang again. This time it was my link worker Becky.

'Right, Maggie, I've got a carer who can do respite at your house,' she told me.

'That's brilliant,' I gushed. 'I can't believe you've found someone so quickly.'

'Her name's Carol Bingley,' she continued.

'Oh, I know Carol,' I said. 'She only lives round the corner from me and I've met her at a few coffee mornings and training sessions. Her husband Dave's a plumber and she's got a teenage son who's at catering college?'

'Yes, that's the one,' replied Becky. 'She's a really lovely lady.'

I pictured the down-to-earth blonde woman in her late forties. She was warm and friendly, and I knew she would be a calming presence for the children.

'She's only got one placement at the moment and he's seventeen and at school during the day so she can help you out as and when you need her,' added Becky. 'I've passed on your number so she's going to give you a call later on.'

'Great,' I sighed, relieved. 'In that case, I'd better phone the school and see if they can take Mary then.'

The local primary school was a ten-minute walk from my front door. I'd been sending foster children there for years and I had a good relationship with the head teacher, Mrs Moody. 'Looked-after children', as kids in the care system were referred to, always got priority, so even if the class was full they'd still have to find a place for Mary.

That afternoon I gave her a ring.

'Maggie!' she exclaimed. 'I haven't heard from you for ages. How are you?'

'Tired,' I laughed. 'So no change there.'

'How can we help you?' she asked.

'I've got three children who have just come to live with me who need school places.'

I told her their ages.

'What's the possibility of the eight-year-old girl starting by the end of the week?' I asked. 'I could bring her in the day after tomorrow for a look round and to meet her teacher?'

'I'm sure we can sort something out,' she said. 'But what about the boys?'

'I think I need a little bit more time with them,' I explained. 'I wanted to get Mary sorted first, then perhaps we could look at a staggered start for them the week after.'

'Of course,' she replied. 'Just let me know how it's going and when you want them to start and we'll see you the day after tomorrow with Mary.

'It'll be nice to have you back in the school community, Maggie. We've missed you.'

My last few placements had been with older children so I hadn't had any involvement with the primary school for a while.

That evening Carol rang and I told her all about the children.

'Becky gave me a bit of background,' she said when I'd finished. 'The way some adults treat their children is just horrendous. It sounds like they were left to live like wild animals,' she sighed.

'They were,' I told her. 'I'm not going to lie to you, Carol. They've very damaged children and they're a handful. They're quite wild so when we're in one room I tend to lock us in so they can't go charging off around the rest of the house.'

'Goodness me, it's that bad?' she asked.

'I'm getting there,' I sighed. 'Slowly but surely.

'In an ideal world I wouldn't be leaving them with anyone else at this early stage, but their social worker wants them in school and I think Mary's the most ready. Once I get her sorted then I can try and work on the boys.'

'You're not a miracle worker, Maggie,' said Carol kindly. 'None of us are, so don't beat yourself up about it. You're just doing the best you can for these kids.'

She was right. It took more than a few days to erase a lifetime of neglect. Maybe we were expecting too much too soon from these children?

I arranged for Carol to come round the following day, just for half an hour.

'I think it would be good for you to meet them before I leave them the following day,' I said. 'I'm going to take Mary up to school and then afterwards I'll need an hour to have a quick whizz round the shops with her to get uniform and PE kits.'

'That's fine,' she said.

I didn't want to take the boys as I knew it would be too much of a distraction. There was also a part of me that worried the school would see how badly behaved and out of control they were and not want to take them.

I was nervous about telling the kids about Carol as I wasn't sure how they were going to react. I waited until the following morning.

'My friend Carol's coming round today,' I told them as I cleared away the breakfast dishes. 'She really wants to meet you as sometimes she might look after you for a little while when I've got to go out and do things.'

'Don't like Carol,' sneered Sean.

'Do we have to go and live with Carol?' asked Mary, looking anxious.

'No, lovey, Carol's coming round here,' I reassured her. 'In fact, in a couple of days Carol's going to come round and look after the boys for a couple of hours because you and I are going to go and visit your new school.'

'School?' asked Mary, a puzzled look on her face. 'Why do I have to go to school?'

'So you can meet other children your age and make some friends,' I explained. 'You'll learn how to read and write and that means that you can read books all by yourself. Does that sound OK?'

'Will you come with me?' she asked, a concerned look on her face.

'Of course I will.' I smiled. 'We'll meet your new teacher and see your classroom. It will be really exciting.'

'Where is it?' she wondered.

'It's literally just up the road and we can walk there every morning and walk back every afternoon,' I said.

I knew it was a lot for her to take in and I could see Mary was trying to get her head around the idea.

I'd asked Carol to come round at lunchtime as the boys tended to be more amenable and quieter when there was food involved.

She was as warm and friendly as I'd remembered. The boys were playing outside when she arrived so she chatted to Mary.

'You must be very excited about going to school.' Carol smiled.

'Yes, Maggie said there might be some other girls my age for me to play with,' Mary told her shyly. I was relieved that she seemed to be slowly warming to the idea.

When the boys came running in, Carol introduced herself.

'This must be Dougie and Sean,' she exclaimed. 'I'm Carol. It's nice to meet you.'

Dougie ignored her and started bouncing on the sofa.

Sean looked her up and down.

'I can see your boobies,' he told her. 'Are you going to show us your boobies?'

Carol was wearing a V-neck top but it wasn't low cut by any stretch of the imagination. If she was shocked, she hid it well.

'I don't think you can see my boobs,' she told him matter-of-factly. 'Well, at least I hope you can't.'

'I'm sorry about that,' I sighed when Sean had wandered off. 'We're having a few issues with oversexualised behaviour.'

We had a cup of coffee while the kids played and I talked a bit about their background.

'They've never had anyone telling them what to do, when to eat, when to sleep, so they haven't had any boundaries,' I explained. 'There were no regular meals on the table so it was grabbing what they could when they could and they went to the toilet wherever they wanted.'

'Poor little mites,' murmured Carol, her eyes filling up with tears. 'How any parent can let their children live like that beggars belief.'

I explained how since they'd come to live with me they'd had a very rigid routine.

'They're only allowed to eat if they're sat nicely at the table,' I told her. 'I've been very strict on please and thank yous.'

I also explained about toilet-training the boys and how I set a timer for them to go to the toilet every ten minutes.

'Even if they don't do anything I get them to sit there and try,' I said.

As if on cue, Dougie came wandering into the kitchen.

'I need a piss,' he said.

'A what?' I said. 'Do you mean a wee or a pee?'

He nodded.

'Thank you for telling me, Dougie. That's brilliant.'

I was so pleased that he was getting the hang of it and left Carol to keep an eye on Mary and Sean while I took him to the bathroom.

★

Now that the children had met Carol, I felt a lot more reassured, but I couldn't help but worry about leaving the boys with her in case they kicked off. When she arrived the following morning I didn't make a big deal about leaving.

'I'm just going to pop out with Mary and I'll be back in a bit,' I told the boys. 'Carol's here and she knows where everything is and I've shown her the juice and the biscuits. Do you think you can show her the sandpit in the garden?'

I wanted to distract them so they didn't actually see Mary and I leave.

Carol must have sensed my worry.

'They'll be fine,' she told me, giving my hand a sympathetic pat.

'I've got my mobile with me in case of any problems,' I replied.

Mary was very quiet on the walk to school and I could tell she was nervous. I chatted to her all the way in a bid to reassure her.

'The school is so close, you'll be able to see it in a minute,' I said brightly.

Mrs Moody was as lovely and reassuring as ever. She was in her late fifties and had been a teacher for over thirty years so she was very experienced. She had a kind and gentle manner but also didn't take any nonsense.

'Hello, Mary.' She smiled, greeting us at reception. 'Maggie's told me all about you and we're looking forward to you joining us tomorrow.'

Leading us into the building, she introduced Mary to her new teacher who was a very sweet young woman called Miss Gandy whom I could tell Mary was instantly smitten with.

'Miss Gandy's going to show you your new classroom for ten minutes while Maggie and I have a chat,' Mrs Moody explained.

Mary hesitated and looked at me. I could see the fear in her eyes.

'Go on.' I smiled encouragingly. 'You can go and have a look at all the books and meet some of the other girls.'

Mrs Moody and I had a quick chat in her office.

'She seems like a sweet girl,' she said.

'She is,' I agreed. 'She's the easiest one of the three. There might be a bit of swearing but it's more learnt behaviour than anything else.

'The boys are not as compliant,' I sighed. 'I'm still in the process of toilet-training them so hopefully I'll have got that sorted by the time that they start.'

'Do what you can, Maggie,' she reassured me. 'We'll just take it as it comes.'

When I went to collect Mary from her classroom, she came skipping out.

'See you tomorrow, Mary,' Miss Gandy smiled and Mary waved.

'What did you think?' I asked her as we walked out of the school gates.

'It was good.' She beamed. 'You were right, there are other girls and I've got a table to sit at and a book that I write something in and Miss says I can choose a story book to read.'

'That sounds brilliant,' I laughed.

'Will the boys come to my school too?' she asked excitedly.

'I hope so.' I smiled. 'But we need to make sure they can both do wees and poos in the toilet first.'

'Yeah,' she sighed. 'I don't think no one at my school wears pull-ups.'

I'd asked Carol to watch the boys for a couple of hours so that I could take Mary to the shops to buy a few things for school. We jumped on the bus and went to Marks & Spencer where I picked up some white polo shirts and grey skirts, a PE kit and let Mary choose a lunch box and bag. I watched Mary like a hawk to make sure she wasn't taking anything she shouldn't, but she just seemed excited, and insisted on carrying the shopping bags once we'd paid.

'I've never had no uniform before.' She smiled.

'I've already got some special school jumpers at home so I'll get one out for you for tomorrow,' I told her.

'Can you show me when we get back?' she asked, practically jumping up and down with excitement.

On the walk home from the bus stop we passed a little park.

'Swings!' she gasped. 'Can I go on them?' she pleaded.

'Go on then.' I smiled. 'Quickly, though, because remember we've got to get back to Carol and the boys.'

Mary ran over to one of the swings but when she got there she stopped.

'Do you know how to do it yourself?' I asked her.

She shook her head.

'Sit on it then and hold onto the ropes and I'll give you a push.'

It was wonderful to see her face when I pushed her higher and higher into the air. I realised it was the first time I had seen her look happy.

'Ooh,' she laughed. 'I went so high my tummy felt funny.'

I felt mean asking her to come off but I knew we needed to get back as I was worried about how things were at home.

As we were walking down the street, she was suddenly very quiet. She stopped and her eyes glazed over.

'Maggie, where's my mummy?' she asked in a quiet voice.

My heart broke at her innocent question and the hopefulness in her voice. It was as if she'd had the sudden realisation that she hadn't seen her mum in a long while. I couldn't understand what had happened. A few minutes ago she was smiling and happy on the swing. Is that what had triggered her memory?

'Was it the swings that reminded you of Mummy?' I wondered. 'Did you used to go to the park with her?'

She nodded her head sadly.

'When I was little, a long time ago,' she sighed. 'Mummy had to meet some man in the park and she brang me. We played on the swings.'

I wasn't sure what her mum had been doing in the park but at least she had a positive memory of her. As we walked along I held her hand and tried as best as I could to explain where her parents were.

'Your mummy and daddy are living in a special building that the police look after,' I told her gently. 'They're safe and it means the police can talk to them whenever they want and when the police have finished talking to them, then they'll work out where they're going to live.'

'What you mean they're banged up?' she asked.

She must have seen my shocked expression. 'I'm eight, Maggie, I know all about prison. Dad's been banged up before but Mummy normally gets off with a caution. Did someone grass them up?'

I was stunned. I'd been trying to protect her by using childlike language and phrasing things in a gentle way but she clearly had a concept of prison and knew what it meant. I knew I had to be honest with her.

'Yes, sweetie, they are in prison,' I sighed. 'When the police have finished talking to them a judge will decide whether they have to stay in prison or not.'

'OK.' She nodded. 'So they're not coming back?'

'Not for a while, no,' I replied.

As I put my key into the front door, my worries switched from Mary to how the boys had been for Carol. She looked a lot more dishevelled than she had been when we left her but she was still smiling.

'I think I need to go home for a lie-down,' she laughed.

'Have they been OK?' I asked her anxiously.

'You were right, Maggie – they didn't give me a minute. If I wasn't lifting them off various items of furniture or pulling them off each other, I was taking them to the toilet.'

When Dougie saw that I was back, he came running over to me, straddled my leg and started rubbing himself up and down. My heart sank. It was horrifically sad that a child his age thought that simulating sex was the way to show someone affection. I'd been keeping a close eye on things and in my opinion I didn't think the children had been showing any other signs that they'd been sexually abused. But they needed to understand the difference between appropriate and inappropriate behaviour. All I could keep doing was reinforcing this and hopefully they would eventually learn.

I peeled him off me.

'Hello, Dougie, I've missed you too,' I told him, smiling.

Mary was busy showing Carol her PE kit and all her new school stuff.

'Guess what?' she told her, once she'd emptied out the shopping bags. 'Maggie says our mum and dad are in prison.'

'Oh,' said Carol, glancing up at me with raised eyebrows, clearly taken by surprise at her honesty. 'I'm sorry to hear that.'

After we'd said goodbye to Carol I kept the rest of the day very quiet as I could see all the children were exhausted. I wanted to keep things low-key as I knew Mary had a big day ahead of her tomorrow.

That night I gave her a bubble bath.

'How about I put your hair in plaits in the morning for school?' I suggested. 'Would you like that?'

She nodded.

I hoped she would get a good night's sleep but when I went to check on her just before 9 p.m. she was still wide awake. Dougie and Sean were thankfully out for the count.

I went and sat on her bed.

'Are you OK, lovey?' I asked her.

She nodded, not looking at me.

'Try and get some sleep as you're going to have such an exciting day tomorrow . . . Night night,' I soothed, stroking her hair and pulling the covers up.

'Maggie, why do you always say that?' she asked suddenly.

'Say what?' I replied, confused.

'Why do you always say to us "night night" and not "f**k off" like our mummy did?'

I tried to hide my shock.

'Because I don't like those words,' I explained. 'They're not very kind words to say to someone you care about. I much prefer saying "night night". Do you?'

Mary nodded thoughtfully and snuggled down under the sheets.

As I pulled her bedroom door closed, I felt tears pricking my eyes. It was her genuine confusion that had got to me the most. She couldn't understand why I didn't swear at her every night. This had been this poor child's reality; this was what she was used to. And frankly, it was heartbreaking.

SEVEN

Testing Times

Sometimes, despite your best efforts, things just turn to chaos. The boys were running round the house, naked and screeching, while I hurriedly helped Mary into her new school uniform.

'Good girl,' I told her, trying not to panic as I looked at the clock. 'You get your jumper on while I see to the boys and then I'll do your plaits.'

We'd all been up since 6 a.m. but, perhaps sensing a change in the usual routine, Dougie and Sean had been particularly wild. They'd ripped their pyjamas off but were refusing to get dressed. First I had to catch them and then wrestle them into their clothes while Mary looked on anxiously. I could tell she was nervous about school and I had wanted to make the morning as calm as possible. Her brothers, however, had other ideas. By the time we left the house, I felt like a broken woman.

As we walked along the street to school, I gripped the boys' hands tightly so there was no chance of them running off. I felt guilty as I'd been so busy trying to get them ready that

I'd hardly had much chance to reassure Mary, although I'd hurriedly plaited her hair as promised. As we walked into the noisy, crowded playground, she stopped dead in her tracks. I could see the fear in her eyes.

'Oh look, there's Miss Gandy,' I said cheerfully. 'Let's go over and say hello.'

'What if I don't like it, Maggie?' she whispered, her big blue eyes wide with panic.

'I'm sure you're going to love it, sweetie,' I reassured her, squeezing her hand.

'Let's go and see Miss Gandy and tell her you're feeling a bit worried.'

Thankfully, the young teacher couldn't have been nicer.

'You're going to have a great day, Mary,' she smiled at her. 'Say bye bye to Maggie, then I'll introduce you to Evie who's going to be sitting on the same table as you.'

As Miss Gandy held out her hand Mary took it and turned round and gave me a weak smile.

'See you soon, lovey.' I waved.

I'd been so worried about the boys running off in the play-ground or causing a scene but both of them were unusually quiet and clingy. I could see they were unsure of this strange place called school and what it meant.

Dougie clung to my leg like a limpet and Sean edged closer and closer to me until he was pressed into my side.

As Mary disappeared off into the classroom, Dougie turned to me with a worried look on his face.

'Mary gone?' he whispered.

'She's just gone to school but she'll be back later, lovey,' I told him gently.

'Mary back later,' he repeated as if to reassure himself of the fact.

I could see they were getting anxious and I had never seen them both walk so quickly. I talked to them all the way back to try and keep them calm.

'I know, let's play a game. Who can spot our front door?'

Between them Dougie and Sean pointed out practically every single front door we passed.

'Not yet.' I smiled. 'Keep on looking.'

'There!' said Sean excitedly as we approached my house. 'That's our door.'

'You're right.' I smiled. 'We're here.'

Both boys seemed to be relieved to be back in the safety of the house, but even when we got home they were extremely quiet. It was interesting for me to see how much security Mary provided for them.

'Where's Mary?' Dougie kept asking.

'She's gone to school, remember,' I reminded him. 'We'll go and pick her up after lunch.'

I knew he had no concept of school and it was a tricky thing to explain. I wanted to get them thinking about it because it wouldn't be long before they would be going as well. So I read them a couple of books about school and we watched an episode of *Topsy and Tim* about their first day at school.

Although I'd reassured the boys, I spent the morning worrying about how Mary was getting on. At lunchtime I couldn't stop myself from ringing the school to check. I got through to Angela, the school secretary, who knew me.

'I'm sure she's OK, but I'll pop and see what she's doing right now.'

She called me straight back.

'She's absolutely fine,' she reassured me. 'She's sitting with two other girls and they're all eating their packed lunches together and chattering away.'

'That's brilliant,' I sighed, feeling my stomach sinking with relief. 'Thanks for checking.'

I also called Lisa the social worker to update her.

'Mary went off to school this morning,' I told her. 'She went in fine.'

'That's great news,' she said. 'You see, Maggie? You were worried about nothing. What about the boys?'

'I'm not quite there with them yet,' I replied. 'I need a few more days with them at least. You'll be pleased to know the toilet-training's going well though.'

Amazingly we'd had no accidents at all that day although I shouldn't have spoken too soon. I came off the phone to Lisa and walked into the kitchen where the most horrendous stench hit my nostrils. I knew instantly what it was. It was like a hideous game of hide and seek as I looked in cupboards, under cushions and behind furniture trying to find out where the smell was coming from. I soon found out when I pulled back the curtains to find a steaming pile of poo

I had no doubt that the culprit was Sean, who was still struggling with toilet-training. I got my rubber gloves and bleach and cleaned it up and then went out into the garden to talk to him. I got there just in time to see him weeing in the sandpit.

'Sean, you know you wee in the toilet and not in the sandpit,' I told him firmly. 'If you do it in there, you won't be able to play in it any more. I've just cleaned up your other mess in the kitchen. You need to do your wees and poos in the toilet, please.'

He wasn't in the least bit embarrassed; it was just what he was used to doing and it was a hard habit to break.

That afternoon we went to pick up Mary. She came skipping out with a big smile on her face and Miss Gandy gave me the thumbs up.

'Where have you been?' Sean demanded.

'I've been to my new school,' she told him proudly.

'How was it?' I asked. 'Did you like it?'

She nodded her head and grinned.

'You were right, Maggie, it was really fun. There was other girls there who are eight too. I was sat next to one called Evie and she told me about *My Little Pony*. Can I watch it too?'

'Yes of course.' I smiled. 'I'll see if I can get the DVD for you.'

I was both delighted and relieved her day had gone well although I was exhausted at the thought of doing it all again tomorrow. To my relief the next few days went by without a hitch. The boys got into a routine during the day, and Mary seemed to be settling in well. But on the fourth day Miss Gandy was waiting for me after school, along with a sullen-looking Mary.

'I'm afraid we had a bit of an incident today,' she said grimly.

She explained that Mary had tripped over another girl's foot.

'Unfortunately, Mary got very cross and she pulled the girl's hair quite hard so she's spent the afternoon in another classroom with a teaching assistant in order to calm down.'

'Mary, you know we don't pull people's hair,' I sighed.

'It wasn't my fault,' she shouted. 'She hurt my f***ing leg.'

'Watch your language please,' I reminded her, raising my eyebrows apologetically at her teacher. 'I'm sure Miss Gandy doesn't want to hear you swearing.'

On the way home I tried to chat to her about the incident.

'If you hurt people, then they won't want to play with you,' I explained. 'If you get cross about something you need to tell your teacher what's happened and how you're feeling. You need to have kind hands.'

'OK,' she sighed begrudgingly. 'But she deserved it.'

As the days went on, Lisa continued to chase me about when the boys were going to be starting school.

'I'm doing all I can but I honestly don't think they're ready yet,' I told her.

I was struggling to get my head around how they were even going to be toilet-trained by that point, never mind emotionally ready for all the challenges school brought.

But Dougie surprised me and by halfway through the second week with me, he was dry and also slightly calmer in his behaviour. So Carol came round and looked after Sean while I took Dougie down to school to meet his new teacher, Mrs Wilson. As he was going into reception, his days would mainly be about play and after seeing his new classroom, he couldn't wait to start playing with all the toys. Lisa had agreed that, because of his age, we could ease him in with a week of mornings to start off with before staying the whole day. On his first morning I sent him in with a big bag of spare trousers and pants and a request that the teaching assistant should keep reminding him to go to the toilet. He came out clutching a bag of wet clothes but more importantly with a big smile on his face.

'Maggie!' he yelled, tearing across the playground towards me. 'I love school. It was f***king brilliant!'

It was another one of those moments when I wanted the ground to swallow me up as all the other school mums turned to stare.

'I'm really pleased you enjoyed it, lovey, but let's try not to use the f-word,' I said quietly.

It was just Sean and me at home now and to my surprise, he was very different without his brother and sister there: he was a lot quieter, less boisterous and a lot more manageable.

I started to do activities with him that involved sitting down and making things with Play-Doh, and making pictures by sticking and gluing. Up until now, the only time I could convince him to sit down at the table was for food, but I knew that when he did go to school he'd be expected to sit down for most of the day, so I wanted him to get used to it. He even managed to do a little bit of drawing and painting – something I could never have attempted with him even a few days ago.

As the two-week deadline drew to a close, Lisa came down heavy on me.

'He's not ready,' I pleaded with her.

'The school will just have to cope with the toilet issue,' she sighed, exasperated. 'It's a legal requirement that he's in full-time education, Maggie.'

'It's not just the toilet-training,' I explained. 'I don't think he's ready emotionally. If we send him now it's not going to go well.'

'That's a chance we'll have to take,' she told me firmly.

So reluctantly, I arranged with Mrs Moody for Sean to start the following week. Beforehand I took him to meet his new teacher Mrs Webster and look round his classroom like the others had. I'd left him for five minutes while I talked to Mrs Moody in her office when the door flew open and Sean stamped in.

'I've saw it, Maggie,' he growled at me defiantly. 'We can go back now. I don't like it. I ain't going to school.'

'I'm afraid you'll have to, lovey. Dougie and Mary go to school and you have to as well.'

A few seconds later Mrs Webster came dashing into the room looking very flustered.

'I'm so sorry about that,' she exclaimed, apologising profusely. 'I took my eye off him for a second to help another child and he just ran off.'

'It's OK,' I reassured her. 'I'm going to take Sean home now and we'll see you on Monday.'

I didn't talk about school again. If Sean wanted to talk about it, that was fine, but I didn't want to ram it down his throat. I wanted Sean to understand that home and school were separate, and for my house to feel like a safe place for him. It was the only security he had and I didn't want to keep bringing up school and upsetting him.

That weekend, Sean was wilder than ever. He was constantly fighting with Dougie and tormenting him. On Sunday, he nearly smashed the patio doors by throwing a pan at them.

'Is he really going to be OK going to school on Monday?' asked Louisa doubtfully.

'Their social worker has made it perfectly clear that he'll have to be,' I sighed, shaking my head.

'I just pity his poor teacher,' groaned Louisa.

I deliberately didn't talk about school all weekend. I knew I needed to present it to Sean as a fait accompli – this was what was happening. Monday morning was a nightmare. We'd been making good progress and over the last week, I'd taught the boys how to dress themselves. Now it was like Sean had gone backwards. I physically had to hold him down to get him dressed into his uniform.

'No, no, no, I don't want to,' he yelled, running down the landing.

Mary, bless her, tried her best to reassure him.

'Sean, school's OK,' she told him. 'The teachers are nice and you can do drawing and learn to read and stuff. Dougie likes it too.'

But he didn't even acknowledge her as he tore up and down the stairs.

In the end I had to resort to the ice-pop trick as I desperately needed to get him out of the house by 8.45 a.m.

I practically had to drag him down the street to school. I waved the other two off into their classrooms, then took Sean to his, where Mrs Wilson was waiting.

'Right, I'll see you later,' I said firmly. 'Have a brilliant day.'

'No,' he screamed. 'Don't want to go.'

He fell to the floor where he kicked and screamed and rolled around.

'Maggie, you go,' Mrs Wilson told me. 'He'll be fine. I'm sure he'll calm down when you've gone.'

I felt awful leaving him but I knew I had to. An hour later Mrs Wilson rang me.

'I'm so sorry to call you, Maggie, but I really think you need to pick Sean up. We haven't managed to calm him down and he's disrupting the whole class. He hasn't stopped screaming and shouting since you left.'

My heart sank and I felt so guilty. When I went to collect him, I could see that he was beside himself. His hair was wet with sweat and his voice was hoarse from all the shouting.

'Let's go home, sweetie,' I told him gently.

'I hate you, Maggie,' he croaked. 'I ain't coming back with you.'

I could see he was furious at me for leaving him there. I tried the only tactic that I knew would work with him – the promise of food.

'That's such a shame because I'm about to go home and have some cheese on toast and an apple because it's lunch time and I'm really hungry.'

That was enough for him to give in. I held out my hand to him and begrudgingly he took it. When we got home, I got him a drink of juice and he sat on the sofa while I made lunch. When I looked over at him five minutes later, he was fast asleep.

He looked so small and peaceful and I felt so sorry for this bewildered little boy. It was so much harder for him. Mary was a lot more advanced than her brothers, and Dougie was at the age where his peers had only just started school, so he wasn't the odd one out. But Sean was with other seven-year-olds who'd been going to school for three years, while he had no idea how to behave.

Tomorrow we'd try again but the morning had only confirmed my fears that Sean wasn't ready to cope with school.

Over the next few days I persevered, but I was up and down to the school like a yoyo. Sometimes Sean lasted three hours, sometimes Mrs Wilson called me after an hour. He refused to sit down at a table, he swiped books and paper off the desks and kicked chairs over. He wandered around the classroom, poking other children, touching things or knocking them over. He wasn't allowed out at playtime because he would try to climb over the school gates.

On his third day Mrs Moody pulled me aside at drop-off.

'Sean's got to get used to staying the whole day,' she told me. 'I'm also aware that we can't keep ringing you to come and collect him. So I've got a teaching assistant who's going to work with him in a separate classroom to see if that helps him feel more settled.'

'Thank you,' I told her gratefully. 'I know he's causing a lot of disruption.'

I hoped in time that he would calm down. Every day Mrs Moody rang me just before pick-up to update me on how he'd been.

'He stayed in the classroom with the TA but apparently spent most of the day sitting under the table,' she told me.

'Do you think there's any chance of trying to find him a different chair to sit on?' I asked her. 'I think he might feel more secure on one with sides.'

'It's worth a try,' she replied.

I was so grateful to her and the school for being willing to stick it out. I knew many schools would have just given up and said they couldn't take him.

Thankfully, after a couple of weeks of seemingly never-ending battles, things slowly started to settle down. I wouldn't go as far as to say Sean was enjoying school, but he had begun to tolerate it. He'd built a good relationship with the TA and he didn't seem to feel so overwhelmed going into a classroom on his own.

He'd been there for a month when Mrs Moody took me to one side on morning after drop-off.

'What is it?' I asked, my heart sinking, I certain it was bad news and that Sean was being asked to leave.

'It's nothing to worry about, Maggie.' She smiled. 'Quite the opposite in fact. Sean's behaviour has improved enough that we feel he's ready to be moved back into the classroom with the other children.'

'That's brilliant.' I grinned, sighing with relief.

'I think we've turned a corner with him at last,' she said. 'It's onwards and upwards from here.'

I smiled, desperately hoping that she was right. The last few weeks had been hell with these children, but now maybe things were finally changing.

EIGHT

Turning a Corner

Soon it was time for the six-week review, to be held at my house while the children were at school. Becky, my link worker, came round, as well as Lisa and Mrs Moody, the head teacher from school. The meeting was chaired by the Independent Reviewing Officer, a woman called Julie. The IRO was someone who worked for Social Services but who wasn't involved in this particular case. Julie was in her fifties and a lovely woman who I'd worked with several times before. She'd been the social worker for a couple of children that I'd previously fostered and I had a lot of respect for her.

'Maggie, it's great to see you.' She smiled. 'It sounds like you've got your hands full with this placement.'

'I certainly have,' I agreed, grinning.

Julie introduced us all and Lisa gave everyone a bit of background on the children and why and when they'd come into the care system.

'There are no suitable family or friends able to take them and at this point in time, neither parent is putting up any objection to the children remaining in care,' she told us.

'In fact, Mum and Dad seem to have no desire whatsoever to have any contact with the children,' she added.

'I've tried to give them information about the kids and how they're doing but to be honest they were both completely disinterested.'

'That's upsetting,' sighed Julie, shaking her head.

Although it was something I'd encountered a lot during my time as a foster carer, it was still so unbearably sad when parents had so little interest and concern for their own flesh and blood.

'Where are their parents now?' asked Becky.

'They're still on remand,' said Lisa. 'They've both pleaded not guilty to the drug offences so they're awaiting a trial date and are both going to be in prison for the foreseeable future.'

'And how are you getting on with the children, Maggie?' asked Julie, turning to me.

'If I'm being honest, it's been an intense six weeks,' I told her.

'But all three of them are now in full-time school and are blossoming,' Lisa interjected proudly.

'I would say they're managing.' I frowned, correcting her as politely as I could. 'But as they've never been in education before, it's been a big challenge for them. Sean has struggled the most – academically, socially and with his behaviour – but I'm hopeful that things will improve. I'm sure Mrs Moody can update you in more detail.'

Mrs Moody went through each child and how they'd settled in.

'I'm sure Maggie will agree with me when I say that both Mary and Dougie have come on in leaps and bounds.' She smiled.

'They love school,' I agreed, nodding. 'Mary skips in happily every morning and comes home talking about her friends and what they've done that day. Dougie's the same and wants to invite the whole class home for tea so I've had to rein him in a bit as I don't think I've got the room,' I laughed and everyone chuckled.

Mrs Moody explained how, although Mary was behind academically, she was picking things up quickly.

'She's already made great progress in reading and literacy and she loves stories,' she said.

Everyone's major concern was Sean.

'Sean is finding it hard,' sighed Mrs Moody. 'We set him up with a teaching assistant in another classroom and that seems to have calmed him down. He comes back into the main classroom for some lessons such as art, but he does get very frustrated when it comes to maths and literacy as he hasn't got the understanding. Unfortunately he's at an age where he knows that he's different and the other children know it too.'

Unlike his siblings, Sean never talked about any of the other pupils and was struggling to make friends.

'Perhaps in the long term we need to look at whether a mainstream school is the best place for him?' suggested Julie.

'It's hard to know at this point,' said Mrs Moody. 'It could be that he just needs more time to settle than Mary and Dougie.'

I really hoped that was the case, as I didn't want to single him out and take him away from his siblings. I knew it gave all three of them a sense of security knowing they were all at the same school.

'So what's the long-term plan looking like at this stage?' asked Julie.

'Well, I've already spoken to Maggie and I know that she's happy to keep fostering them on an ongoing basis,' replied Lisa.

I nodded.

'We're going to go to the courts for a full care order and then perhaps at some point in the future, we can look at whether adoption is an option for them.

'I'll need to speak to the children of course and explain what's happening,' she added.

Everyone was in full agreement that a full care order was the only way forward.

That afternoon after school, Lisa came round to talk to them.

'Everyone, let's sit down and have some juice and a biscuit,' I told them.

'You need to be quick because this is the only time they'll all sit down and listen,' I told her under my breath.

'I wanted to talk to you about your parents,' Lisa told them gently.

None of them showed any reaction. Dougie munched on his biscuit, Mary stared into the distance and Sean slid down his seat and sat on the floor under the table. I knew he was still listening so I didn't tell him to get back up.

'Your mummy and daddy don't feel able to see you at the moment,' Lisa continued.

'Are they still in prison?' asked Mary matter-of-factly.

'Er yes,' replied Lisa, looking startled. 'Yes, I'm afraid that they are. So I wanted to let you know that you're going to be staying with Maggie for a while. Does that sound OK?'

Mary bit into her biscuit and didn't show any reaction. Sean was quiet under the table.

'But can we stay in this house and still go to the same school?' asked Dougie anxiously.

'Yes, sweetie, you'll all be staying at this house and you'll keep going to your school,' I reassured him.

He looked relieved.

'Has anyone got any more questions?' asked Lisa.

'I do!' shouted Dougie. 'I've got a friend called Alfie and he likes tractors just like me. Can I take a tractor into school to show him tomorrow?'

'Er yes, I'm sure Maggie will let you do that,' Lisa told him, looking slightly confused at the change of subject.

I knew each of the children would process this information in their own way in their own time.

A few minutes later the biscuits had been eaten and they were itching to leave the table.

'Can we go and play?' asked Mary.

'Go on then.' I nodded.

Lisa had told them all she needed to.

'They don't seem in the least bit perturbed or upset about Mum and Dad not wanting to see them,' sighed Lisa once they'd left.

'I think Mary will be, but sadly the boys don't seem to have any interest or attachment to their parents. They haven't asked about them once.

'I think their security is Mary,' I continued. 'She's the glue that holds them all together.'

When Lisa had gone, I sat at the kitchen table and finished off my cup of tea while I watched the children play outside in the garden. I was relieved that they were staying with me for the time being. They were very damaged and confused children and I was determined to make a difference and do my best for them. All I could hope was that we were through the worst of it.

'Onwards and upwards,' I sighed to myself, finishing off the dregs of my tea. 'Onwards and upwards.'

Some greater entity must have heard my plea because over the next few months things did slowly start to change. School had really helped the children. It had given them structure and routine which in turn made them feel safe and secure. They'd gone from being feral creatures who did whatever they wanted, whenever they wanted, to really relishing rules and boundaries. Outside school, I kept things very rigid, quiet and home-based as I knew it was exactly what they needed. In fact, when things veered away from their normal routine it really distressed them and made them anxious.

One day at school it had been warm and sunny, so Mary's teacher Miss Gandy decided to do their afternoon lessons outside. At home time when I went to pick up the children, she took me to one side.

'I'm afraid Mary was involved in a fight with another girl,' she said. 'It's so unlike her, but this afternoon she's been really difficult and argumentative.'

It was only when she told me about the outdoor lesson that I put two and two together.

'I'm not trying to make excuses for her behaviour, but she was probably feeling anxious because her normal routine had changed,' I explained.

Without the structure and security of a routine, I knew Mary would feel out of control. I was concerned it might have also triggered memories of the past for her.

At first, it was just little things that I noticed improving. To my relief, their anxiety about food had slowly started to ease. One afternoon I went to make them some toast after school but when I opened the cupboard, I realised there was only one slice left.

'Oh no,' I sighed. 'We're out of bread.'

I registered the look of absolute horror and fear on Sean's face.

'Well, come on then,' I told them breezily. 'Let's all get our shoes on and walk to the shop and we can get a loaf of bread.'

'What, you can just get another one?' asked Sean, amazed.

'Yes, lovey, when things run out, we can go and buy a new one,' I reassured him.

When we got to the corner shop I got him to go and choose a loaf off the shelves and I gave him the money to take to the till. I hoped that he was starting to realise that food was always going to be available.

Another night I was cooking dinner when I forgot about the sausages.

'What's that funny smell?' asked Mary.

I ran to the oven but it was too late.

'Silly me,' I sighed. 'They're burnt to a crisp.'

I saw the worried looks on the children's faces as they watched me remove the charred remains of the sausages from the oven. Dougie looked like he was about to burst into tears and his anxiety was palpable.

'Never mind,' I said. 'Let's just choose something else from the freezer to have with our mashed potato and peas. How about fish fingers instead?' I suggested. 'I can put them in the oven straight away.'

I opened the freezer and showed the kids all the drawers full of food.

'It doesn't matter that the sausages went black does it, Maggie?' said Dougie. 'Cos we've got more.'

'That's right.' I smiled. 'I've got lots of other food in the cupboard and in the fridge and in the freezer.'

I knew if the same thing had happened a few weeks ago it would have caused enough anxiety to trigger a massive meltdown.

The children all took a packed lunch to school as I knew that school dinners would have fuelled their fears. They would have found it hard to queue up and wait their turn and they would worry that they wouldn't get any or that the food might run out. Packed lunches were better because they could actually see me putting the food into them. They loved choosing which sandwich filling and fruit they wanted for the following day.

All three had started becoming picky about their food too. When they'd first arrived, they would have shoved anything in their mouths. Now, however, they were developing their own likes and dislikes – which was sometimes a bit of a pain for me! Dougie had decided he didn't like baked beans any more but he would eat spaghetti hoops. Mary hated cucumber and Sean didn't like eggs but loved green vegetables like broccoli and cabbage.

During the first few weeks with these children I had struggled to keep control of them. Their behaviour had initially been so wild. But I'd stuck with it and given them consistency and routine. It had been exhausting and every day had been a battle, but slowly it seemed to be working. As the months passed, their behaviour was changing and they were becoming more manageable.

I learnt to recognise the danger times, like in the afternoons when they came back from school and I could tell that they were exhausted. I made sure I always had a snack ready and we'd sit and chat about their day. Sean liked books but he was really struggling with reading so I'd give him some earphones and get him to sit and listen to an audiobook. I could see that it relaxed him and he could zone out rather than becoming destructive or angry.

Thankfully neither he nor Dougie felt the need to climb on the furniture or trash a room any more. I'd removed all of the Lego soon after they'd first come to live with me because they tipped it all out and threw it around. But now Sean was calmer, I wanted to see if he was capable of playing with it properly.

'Would you like to do some building with Lego?' I asked him one afternoon and he nodded eagerly.

He sat at the kitchen table, I gave him the box and I held my breath. How long until he got angry and frustrated and hurled the whole lot onto the floor? However, he worked intently, slowly working things out and getting the knack of piecing the fiddly blocks together.

'Look, Maggie, I've built our house,' he grinned after twenty minutes.

As he showed me his wonky model that looked nothing like a house, I couldn't have been more proud: not only because of his building skills but also the fact that he'd referred to it as 'our house'.

'It's absolutely brilliant,' I exclaimed. 'You've done so well.'

'Can I make another one?' he asked.

'Of course you can, sweetie.' I smiled.

The other two were playing with the doll's house, so while Sean was engrossed in the Lego, I took advantage of the peace and quiet and got on with making dinner.

Sean was still hunched over, building away, when Louisa walked in the door from work.

'Hi, Louisa,' he said, looking up. 'Please can you pass me that yellow block that's dropped on the floor? I need it to finish my model.'

'Course I can.' She smiled.

'Thanks.' He beamed, as she put it on the table for him.

She came walking over to me with her eyebrows raised.

'Have I come to the right house?' she whispered, as she put her handbag and keys down on the work surface.

'What do you mean?' I asked, confused.

'Well, I used to come home from work to chaos,' she explained. 'Sometimes I could hear Sean shouting from the street. Now look at him. He's saying please and thank you automatically and he's playing quietly with the Lego. What have you done to him? It's all so *calm.*'

I looked around and surveyed the scene for myself. Louisa was right. There was no screaming or shouting, no one was running round, climbing on the furniture or going to the toilet on the floor.

Dare I say it? Things *were* calm. The manners generally came automatically now without being prompted. Admittedly I was still working on the swearing.

When Sean had finished he was terribly proud of his Lego creations.

'I'm going to put all your models on the shelf so everyone can see them,' I told him. 'You've worked so hard.'

It was lovely to see him smile.

Boosting their self-esteem was one of the many things I was trying to work on. I could see by their utter surprise and delight when I praised them that no one had ever cared for them and they didn't have any sense of self-worth.

Over the past few weeks Mary had become very conscious of her appearance and it made leaving the house a bit of an ordeal.

'Maggie, please can you brush my hair all neat?' she asked me one morning. 'Can you do a braid?'

'We haven't got time today, sweetie,' I apologised. 'But I'll see if Louisa can do one for you tomorrow.'

I was fine with bobbles and clips but Louisa was a dab hand with all the fancier stuff.

Mary asked if she could have some socks with frills on like her friends at school had and she kept asking to have her ears pierced.

'I really like pretty things, Maggie,' she told me.

'What's your favourite colour?' I asked her.

'Pink.' She grinned.

'Oh that's mine too,' I replied enthusiastically. 'Next time I go shopping shall we choose a pink duvet cover for your room?'

'Yes!' she gasped.

I was delighted that she was taking pride in her appearance and starting to care about how she looked. I knew that meant she was happier in herself and that her self-esteem was growing. I wanted her to know that somebody else cared about her too. So we went shopping to the local chemist and she chose some new clips and bobbles and I bought her a pair of frilly socks to match her friends'.

I also asked Lisa if I could take the boys for what I assumed was their first haircut. They both still had shoulder-length hair that was all split and ragged at the ends. Normally I'd have to get parental permission, but Lisa said it would be OK as they were unlikely to raise any objection.

Dougie was so excited about going to the hairdressers.

'Me first, me first,' he begged.

'Go on then.' I smiled, lifting him into the chair. 'You have to stay very still though. Would you like short hair or do you want to keep it longer?'

'Short and spiky,' he said.

He looked like a little prince sitting in the raised seat and he watched intently in the mirror as the hairdresser got to work on his shoulder-length locks.

He giggled as she dried it off with a hairdryer and then rubbed some wax into her hands and ruffled it through his hair.

'Look, Maggie, I've got spikes.' He beamed.

He was absolutely delighted. Sean, however, looked terrified. He cowered on a seat in the corner of the salon, pressing himself up against the wall.

'Your turn, Sean,' I coaxed gently.

'Don't want to,' he hissed. 'Don't want my hair cut.'

'You don't have to have it short like Dougie,' I reassured him. 'You can keep it long if you want and just have a trim.'

I thought it was leading to an almighty meltdown but Sean was so frightened, he didn't say a word. As he sat in the chair I could see him shaking.

'Just do a quick trim please,' I told the hairdresser.

I was so proud of him for getting through it.

'You both look so smart,' I exclaimed afterwards. They were so far removed from the wild, matted creatures that had turned up on my doorstep all those months ago.

When fostering a sibling group it's easy to lump them together at first. But with their behaviour now more under control, I was finding out all about their different likes and dislikes, and their personalities were starting to reveal themselves.

After hearing all about it from their friends, Mary was desperate to go to Brownies and Dougie wanted to go to Beavers in a nearby village hall. I knew Sean wouldn't be able to manage it but I wanted to give him the option and not leave him out.

'Would you like to go to Beavers too?' I asked him.

'No,' he said instantly. 'Don't want to.'

I must admit it was a blessing. Once we'd dropped the other two off, I found I really enjoyed having a couple of hours just with Sean on his own.

One Saturday, Mary and Dougie were at an activity day so I took Sean to a local park that had a butterfly house.

'What are them?' he asked as we walked into the heated greenhouse and he saw all the butterflies flying around.

'They're butterflies,' I explained. 'If you stand very still, one of them might come over to you.'

He loved it when two of them flew over and landed on his arm.

'They're all tickly, Maggie,' he giggled.

'I think they like you.' I smiled.

I could see he was absolutely fascinated and intrigued by them. We took a leaflet about all the different species and when we got home I read it out to him. The next time the others were at Brownies and Beavers, we looked up butterflies on the computer and Sean did some drawings of them. He spent ages colouring them in.

'These are so beautiful,' I gasped as he showed me them, tears of pride pricking my eyes. 'Would you like to go back to the butterfly house again?'

'Can we?' he asked, his face lighting up.

He looked so excited I felt like crying.

The more time I spent with Sean on his own, the more I realised what a sensitive, thoughtful soul he was. He might have been struggling academically and wasn't able to read and write yet, but his brain certainly had the ability to absorb information and he was thirsty for knowledge. By the time we'd visited the butterfly house a couple of times he could identify every single species by name and he knew all about them. I'd bought him a little sketch-pad and pencil and he'd go home and produce the most incredibly detailed drawings.

One afternoon after school Carol came round. We hadn't seen her for a while and I had a few meetings coming up that I needed some respite care for. I thought it would be nice for the children to see her and for us to catch up over a coffee.

'The kids are watching TV in the front room,' I told her when she arrived.

'I'll just pop my head in and say hello to them,' she said.

When she walked back into the kitchen she had a look of pure astonishment on her face.

'I've just had a conversation with all three of them,' she gasped, her eyes wide with surprise.

'What, with the kids?' I smiled. 'Yes, they're proper little chatterboxes these days, aren't they?'

Carol was stunned.

'Maggie, can't you see the difference?' she sighed. 'It's amazing. When they first arrived here I could talk to Mary, but the boys wouldn't keep still. It was all grunts and "no" and "mine". I've just had a lovely chat with Sean about butterflies and Dougie told me all about the painting he did at school today. Their speech has come on so much and there were no f-words either!'

'Yes,' I laughed. 'Thankfully the swearing has been toned down and they're not simulating sex with each other any more.'

I knew that slowly the children were calming down and feeling more settled but I didn't tend to notice the dramatic changes to their behaviour myself because I was with them day to day. It was only when someone else pointed it out that I realised just how far they'd come.

'Maggie, you're a miracle worker,' praised Carol. 'What have you done with those three?'

'I'm afraid there've been no miracles.' I smiled. 'It sounds really dull but I've given them boundaries, consistency and routine.'

'Dull or not, it's bloomin' well worked,' she laughed.

They were only simple things, but if you stuck at them they made such a difference.

Of course there were still blips. We had meltdowns and fights and things were far from perfect. However, we started to do a few social things with other people now too.

One summer's evening my friend Vicky, who was also a foster carer, invited us all to go strawberry-picking at a local farm. She brought her three foster children – six-year-old twin girls Lucy and Erin and three-year-old Jamie. It was a lovely sunny evening and it was idyllic.

The children were amazed not only that all these rows of plants were full of fat juicy strawberries but that they could pick them and eat as many as they wanted.

Vicky and I put a picnic rug on the grass and watched as the kids ran up and down the rows of strawberries. I watched Mary, Dougie and Sean walking along together. They were carefully picking the fruit and putting it in their punnets and then popping the odd one into their mouths.

Suddenly it struck me how far they'd come from the wild children who had rampaged through my house.

'There's no way I could have brought them to do something like this even a couple of months ago,' I said to Vicky. 'They'd have literally crammed every single strawberry into their mouths until they were sick.'

My heart genuinely ached with pride for these three children. They'd been through so much but finally they were coming out the other side.

NINE

Too Much, Too Soon?

As I pushed the trolley up the aisles of the supermarket, the children scampered off in different directions.

'Got the crackers!' yelled Mary, running back.

'I've picked Hobnobs,' said Dougie proudly. 'And Sean's got custard creams.'

'That's brilliant.' I smiled. 'Put them in the trolley and let's tick them off the list then.'

Here we were, four months down the line, and a supermarket trip no longer caused any problems. After their meltdowns the first time round, I'd avoided going to the supermarket with them for months but now we were at a place where all three of them felt secure enough about food that I could allow them to feel more involved. They'd helped me write a list and once we got to Asda they'd go off and get what we needed and put it in the trolley. Even the biscuits didn't cause a problem any more. They all knew they could choose a packet each and then share them during the week.

Summer had now turned to autumn and the children had moved into a new year at school. Thankfully school had become more manageable for Sean and he was able to join in the lessons. There were still times when he felt overwhelmed and angry, but a teaching assistant was always able to step in and move him quickly into another classroom to do something else. He was still struggling socially. He didn't really know how to communicate with children his own age as he hadn't had the same life experiences as them. He didn't know much about the cartoons they mentioned or the different toys they talked about. He was still catching up on Duplo and Lego and wooden train tracks whereas they were into Nintendos and football teams and he found it frustrating and confusing.

We were at a point where behaviourally all three of them had made huge progress. Emotionally, though, I knew it would take them much longer to make secure attachments to people and to be able to show affection. As they had been shown so little by their biological parents, they didn't know how to show love or affection. My belief is that affection should come naturally, it can't be taught or learnt; it's something that's got to come from within and I don't necessarily worry about children not showing me affection. I know they'll do it in their own time when they feel comfortable and I want it to be genuine and not forced. I was naturally affectionate with the kids – I'd put a hand on their shoulder or ruffle their hair – but I'd always ask their permission before I gave them a hug or a kiss goodnight. But so far, none of them had instigated affection with me. It was something I couldn't rush and I hoped that in time it would come.

One night I was watching TV with Mary. She was curled up next to me on the sofa and I was absent-mindedly stroking her hair.

'My mummy didn't do this,' she said suddenly.

'Do what?' I asked.

'Do that to my hair,' she said. 'If I tried to give my mummy a cuddle she told me to f**k off.'

Hearing things like that made me feel desperately sad, but I didn't want to bad-mouth her parents in front of her.

'Oh dear, that's a shame,' I sighed. 'I love my cuddles with you, Mary.'

Another thing the children hadn't done yet was cry. They'd get angry and hit, kick, shout and scream, but they'd never cried actual physical tears. Neglected children often don't cry because sadly they know from experience that if they do, nobody will come, and so gradually they learn not to bother. A similar thing happens with pain. Children often block out any hurt or physical pain because they know there's nobody there to make it better for them. I've fostered children in the past who've had exposed nerves in their teeth or broken bones for months and they've learnt to live with that level of excruciating pain when most adults would be rolling around on the floor in agony. It's heartbreaking to see, but they just switch themselves off and accept it as part of day-to-day life.

One afternoon the children were out playing in the garden when I heard someone screaming. My heart started pounding and I thought something awful had happened.

I rushed out to find Mary shrieking, rolling around on the grass.

'I fell over and hurt my knee,' she sobbed. 'It really, really hurts, Maggie.'

Visions of a hospital trip filled my head and I looked down expecting to see a huge gash in her leg. However, it was a tiny scratch that was barely bleeding. I looked at Mary's distraught face and it was only then that I registered the fat, wet tears streaming down her cheeks.

She was crying!

I knew that allowing herself to cry and register pain was a huge deal for her and it was important that I dealt with her as sympathetically as I could.

'Oh you poor thing,' I soothed. 'Come into the kitchen and I'll sort you out.'

Mary limped inside and I sat her down. I gently patted the cut clean with some cotton wool and put a plaster on it.

'Does that feel better?' I asked, giving her a cuddle. 'You've been so brave.'

'Yes,' she snivelled, dabbing her damp cheeks with the tissue that I'd given her. 'It really, really hurt, Maggie.'

It was the smallest scrape but I wanted to indulge Mary because I wanted her to realise that her life was different now and that somebody did care. If she cried now, somebody would hear her and come.

Crying is also about having empathy and understanding that you've hurt someone else. When older children learn to cry, it's a sign that they're in touch with their emotions and they can recognise that they've done something wrong or they're feeling upset. It all boils down to attachment. As children allow themselves to become emotionally attached to people, it's almost as if they have learnt how to feel.

As the weeks passed I could see that Dougie was also learning to get to grips with his emotions. One weekend the children had been playing and there were toys all over the kitchen floor. I wanted to try and clear it up before we had dinner so I gave them each a job to do.

'Dougie, can you put the train track away please,' I asked him.

Much to my surprise, he burst into tears.

'I didn't get it out,' he sobbed. 'It wasn't me that made the mess. I'm sorry, Maggie.'

I knew he was crying because he thought that he'd let me down. I went over and put my arm around him.

'You don't need to get upset about it, you silly sausage,' I soothed. 'It's only a bit of train track and I'm getting all three of you to help me to tidy up. Did you think I was cross because I thought you'd made the mess?'

He nodded as he dried his tears on his t-shirt. I felt that it was important for him to be able to identify why he was upset.

I chatted to my supervising social worker Becky about it when she called me the following day. She would ring me every week to check how I was and how everything was going.

'It sounds wrong to say that I'm glad the children are crying but I really am,' I laughed.

'It's a good sign,' she agreed. 'It shows they're forming attachments and they feel confident and secure enough with you to be able to show you their emotions.'

'Sean is a different kettle of fish, though,' I sighed. 'I've never seen any tears from him and he still can get so angry.'

'It will come in time,' Becky reassured me.

'Maybe we have to face the fact that it won't,' I told her sadly.

After experiencing trauma and neglect, some children are never able to attach to anyone because they're so damaged by what's happened that they never allow themselves to trust another adult again. It was always such a sad situation and I really hoped it wasn't the case with Sean.

One morning I took the kids to school as normal. Mary's class was always the last one to be called in and I often waited to wave her off.

'Bye, lovey,' I called as she skipped off happily as usual. 'Have a good day.'

Suddenly she stopped dead in her tracks, turned around and ran back to me.

'What is it?' I asked. 'What's wrong?'

'Nothing.' She smiled. 'I just wanted to give you a squish.'

She threw her arms around me, gave me a hug and before I could say another word, she ran off.

'Bye, Maggie, see you later,' she yelled.

I was too shocked to respond as it was the first time she'd given me a hug off her own bat.

After weeks of showing Dougie appropriate ways of giving people affection, he had thankfully stopped rubbing himself up against my leg and would often give me cuddles and although Sean wasn't cuddly at all, he'd press himself against my side if we were sat next to each other and I knew that was his way of showing affection.

One morning I got a call from Lisa to ask if she could come round.

'Of course. The children are at school so I was just catching up with some paperwork. Is there anything in particular that you want to discuss?'

'Oh, I've got a few updates for you and I'd rather chat face to face,' she answered vaguely.

Social workers are always busy, and so normally she would give me a ring to check on the children or to pass on information. I couldn't help but wonder what was so important that she needed to come round.

Later that morning I found out.

'I heard from the CPS yesterday that the children's biological parents had their trial a couple of weeks ago,' Lisa explained.

'They were found guilty and yesterday they were sentenced. Mum got five years and Dad six and a half.'

'Oh gosh,' I sighed. 'They're quite substantial sentences.'

'Yep,' agreed Lisa. 'So they're both going to be in prison at least for the next three years or more. So that leads me to the other thing I wanted to chat to you about.'

I listened intently as Lisa carried on talking.

'Yesterday I had a meeting with my manager and we discussed the fact that the children are likely to be remaining in the care system long term,' she continued. 'I was telling her what an incredible job you've done with them, Maggie.'

'Thank you.' I nodded. 'I can't really take the credit though. It's the children who have done all the hard work.'

'Well, I've seen such amazing changes in them in such a short space of time.' She smiled. 'In fact my manager and I were saying that there's been such a turnaround that we're perhaps at a point where we could start looking for an adoptive family for them.'

'Adoption?' I gasped. 'Now?'

'We would start looking now although it might take quite a few months,' she told me.

It was a complete shock. I'd assumed that because Mary, Dougie and Sean were older and a larger sibling group that adoption wouldn't even be considered.

'What about their ages?' I asked. 'Do you really think you could find someone willing to take on all three kids?'

'My manager said that she was talking to the adoption team the other day and that there were quite a few couples on their books who were interested in older children,' replied Lisa.

I knew there were couples out there who wanted older kids. To adopt children under five, there was an age criteria and some couples in their forties were deemed too old for little ones.

My head was spinning as Lisa explained more.

'So the next step is to bring an adoption social worker out to meet you and the children,' she told me. 'Does that sound OK, Maggie?'

'Er, yes,' I said vaguely, still struggling to get my head around the idea.

'What about their biological parents?' I asked. 'Have you told them the plans?'

'I tried to visit them before they were sentenced but they refused to see me,' said Lisa. 'So I passed the information on via their solicitor and he finally came back to me this morning. Both parents have given their consent and said they wouldn't be contesting the adoption. And before you ask, Maggie, I did ask about a goodbye with the kids but neither of them were interested.'

'That's a real shame,' I sighed.

In my experience goodbyes, no matter how hard or upsetting, helped children to gain some sort of closure and move onto a new family. But it was clear that wasn't what was going to happen in this case.

After Lisa had left, I gave Becky a ring and explained what she'd said.

'I'm a bit shell-shocked to be honest,' I confessed.

'Why?' she asked.

'It just feels so soon,' I sighed. 'These kids have been through so much and they've just started to calm down and get settled.'

'It's been five months,' she told me. 'That's a pretty standard amount of time for Social Services to start looking around for an adoptive family. You and I both know it can take months and they prefer to get things moving rather than having kids languishing in the care system.'

I knew she was right and I was probably just being oversensitive.

'Would you consider adopting them?' asked Becky. 'Is that why you're upset?'

'I honestly don't know,' I sighed. 'I've been thinking about it ever since Lisa left, but my gut feeling is that no matter how much I care about these kids, I would be doing them a disservice if I adopted them.'

I was a single carer and while I had no doubt in my mind that single people made excellent parents, I felt that these children needed two parents. I also knew that boys in the care system needed good male role models and Dougie and Sean in particular would benefit enormously from having a father figure while growing up. I didn't want to deny them that chance.

'You know I believe there's a family out there for every child,' I told Becky. 'And I want these children to get the opportunity of having one of their own. Fostering is my job so I would have to keep doing that and I think these kids need someone who can commit to them and them alone 24–7.'

I felt enormously sad about the possibility of letting them go but part of my role was doing what was in the children's best interests.

'Of course I'm happy to carry on fostering them until they find a suitable family,' I told Becky. 'However long that takes.'

I knew there was also the risk that, because of their age, Social Services might not find someone suitable who was willing to adopt all three of them. But Lisa was clearly deter-mined to get the ball rolling and was keen to tell the children their plans as soon as possible. She'd arranged to come back that night after we'd got back from school.

I wanted to keep everything relaxed and low-key so I hadn't warned them she was coming. When she arrived they were all playing Snap on the kitchen table.

'Put the cards down for now, Mary, while Lisa has a quick chat with you all.' I smiled.

Lisa pulled up a chair and all three looked up at her curiously.

'I wanted to talk to you all to tell you some news,' said Lisa in her best, excited voice.

The children stared at her suspiciously.

'I wanted to let you know that we're going to start looking to see if we can find you a new mummy and daddy. There are lots of forever families out there who are looking for three children just like you to become part of their lives.'

Without taking a pause, she continued: 'Maggie and I know the three of you really, really well now and we want the best possible family that we can find for you. So it might take a long time, but when we've found the right people for you we'll let you know.'

'A new mummy and daddy?' gasped Dougie, his eyes wide with shock. 'But where are you going to find them from? Where will we live? Are we going tomorrow?'

I gave him a cuddle in a bid to try and calm him down and reassure him.

'You're not going anywhere tomorrow.' I smiled. 'It might take months and months. Like Lisa said we've got to find the right family for you.'

Mary was stony-faced.

'So we're never going back to them?' she asked in a quiet voice.

'Who's *them*, Mary?' I asked.

'Our mum and dad who are in prison,' she said. 'We're not going back to them?'

'No, sweetheart, not even if they come out of prison,' I told her gently. 'Does that make you feel sad?'

'No,' she said firmly. 'I didn't like that mum and dad.'

I looked over at Sean who hadn't said a word up until now.

'What do you think, Sean?' I asked him softly. 'How do you feel about it?'

To my shock, he buried his head in his hands and started to cry. His whole body shook with gut-wrenching sobs. Lisa glanced over at me with a look of pure panic.

'What is it, sweetheart?' I asked, reaching over the table to grab his hand.

'Nothing,' he hissed, brushing me off.

It was only when I got up and walked over to him that I saw the puddle of wee under his chair. For the first time in weeks he'd wet himself.

My heart sank. The poor boy looked traumatised. He'd been doing so well these past few weeks but could he really cope with the adoption process and moving to a new family? Or would all the good work we'd done and the progress he'd made suddenly be lost and we'd back to square one? I was suddenly very concerned and I couldn't help but wonder if we were doing the right thing for these children.

TEN

The Search Begins

Pulling his chair out from the table, I put a protective arm around Sean. I could see he was embarrassed about crying in front of everyone and he was rubbing his eyes with his arm.

'Come on, lovey, let's go and get you in some dry trousers and pants,' I told him gently, helping him up.

As we walked upstairs, I could hear Lisa getting Mary and Dougie to draw pictures of the kind of house they wanted their new mummy and daddy to live in.

'I'd like a ginormous house with a pink bedroom!' I heard Mary say.

'I want a doggie and a sandpit like Maggie's got,' piped up Dougie.

Those kinds of activities were good because they got the children used to the idea of going to live in a new place with a new family. It was also useful for social workers to pick up information about the children's likes and dislikes for when they were trying to match them up to potential adopters.

Although Dougie and Mary had seemed to take the news well, Sean looked broken. He sat hunched up on the bed, shaking with fear.

'Oh, sweetheart,' I sighed, sitting down beside him. 'Did the idea of looking for a forever mummy and daddy upset you?'

He looked up at me, his big blue eyes filled with pure fear.

'I don't want to go back,' he whispered. 'I wouldn't like it in a tiny room with bars on the window. You can't make me.'

I realised then that he hadn't quite grasped what Lisa had been telling them.

'You mean you don't want to go back and live with your old mum and dad?' I asked him.

Sean nodded.

'I don't want to live in prison for ever.'

'Sean, lovey, you're not going back to live with them,' I reassured him. 'Social Services wouldn't let you go and live in prison.'

'But Lisa said . . .'

'Lisa is talking about looking for a brand new mummy and daddy for you, Mary and Dougie. We call it a forever family because you go and live with them forever.'

'So I won't have to go and live with the old ones?' he asked, his eyes wide.

'No,' I told him. 'I promise you no one's sending you to live in prison.'

I could see he was really shaken up and my heart broke seeing how afraid he had been. I gave him a cuddle.

'But when do we get the new family?' he asked, confused.

'I'm afraid I don't know that,' I explained. 'Lisa's going to start looking but it can take a long time so at the moment nothing's going to change. You're going to keep on living here with me and Louisa and carry on going to your school,' I continued.

'Then when Lisa does find you a new mummy and daddy, she will let us know.'

Sean still looked worried.

'But what if we don't like the ones she picks?' he asked. 'What if she chooses horrible ones?'

'I bet you will like them.' I smiled. 'Lisa has promised me that she's going to keep looking until she finds the best mummy and daddy there is. She'll go to see them and they'll have to show her how they'd be able to look after you and take care of you. And then you'll meet them. They might come here and have tea with us and you'll be able to play with them and see their house. Lisa will make sure everybody's really, really happy before you go to live with them. Does that sound OK?'

'Suppose so,' sighed Sean, still not looking convinced.

I gave his hand a squeeze.

'Come on, let's get you changed and then we can go back downstairs and see what Mary and Dougie are up to.'

He seemed a little bit more reassured. He put on some clean pants and trousers and we went downstairs.

'I don't want to talk any more,' he told me before we walked into the kitchen. 'I want to play Lego.'

'OK, sweetie,' I told him, ruffling his soft brown hair. 'That's fine.'

While the kids played, Lisa and I had a quick chat in the front room.

'Well, Mary and Dougie seemed to be quite excited about the news,' she told me. 'They had lots of questions and I answered them as best I could. How was Sean?'

'The poor little mite was terrified,' I sighed. 'He didn't quite understand what you were saying and thought he was going back to live with his biological parents in prison.'

'Oh no,' groaned Lisa. 'No wonder he was upset.'

Although I had reassured Sean as best as I could, I knew that he was the one who was going to be the most unsettled at the idea of going to live with a new family.

'Now they know what the plan is they can at least start to get their heads around it,' said Lisa. 'I'll find out who their adoption social worker is going to be and get them to contact you ASAP.'

When Lisa had gone I sat at the kitchen table and had a cup of tea. I was still trying to get used to the idea so I couldn't imagine how it felt for the children. I was still sitting there twenty minutes later when Louisa got in from work. Before I could even open my mouth to tell her the news, Mary came running in from the garden.

'Guess what, Louisa?' she puffed. 'Lisa came round and she's gonna get us a forever mummy and daddy. Not the old ones cos they're banged up, but a new lot and I might even have a pink bedroom.'

'Wow,' gasped Louisa, clearly taken aback. 'That's great.'

When Mary ran back outside she sat down at the table with me.

'So they're going to be adopted?' she questioned. 'It seems so quick. They've just started getting settled and doing OK at school and not pooing all over our floor.'

'I know,' I sighed. 'But Social Services feel they're ready and I can't deny them the chance to have a family of their own.'

Personally I was hoping that it would take a few months to find a prospective couple because I felt the children needed as much time as possible to get used to the idea.

Now that Lisa had told the children what was happening, my aim was to make their forever mummy and daddy part of our normal everyday conversations. I got out my well-worn books about families and how they come in all shapes and sizes and we talked about what kind of house they'd like to live in.

The following Saturday, I was making cheese on toast for lunch.

'Dougie, do you think your forever mummy will know how to make cheese on toast just like you like it with tomato sauce in the middle?'

Dougie grinned.

'She might do,' he said thoughtfully. 'But will you tell her too?'

'Of course, sweetie.' I smiled.

'Will you tell her I don't like beans?' piped up Mary.

'Well you can tell her yourself when you meet her, lovey.'

Throughout all of these chats about forever families and new mummies and daddies, Sean never once joined in.

'What about you, Sean?' I asked him one day. 'What would you like your new mummy and daddy to be like?'

'Stop talking,' he scowled, putting his hands over his ears. 'I'm not listening.'

I left it as I didn't want to push him and I was hopeful that he would open up in his own time.

The following week I got a call from Mrs Moody at the school.

'Before you pick up the children today, would you mind popping into school for a quick word?' she asked me.

'Of course,' I replied, my brain whirring at the thought of what it might be.

When I got to the school, Mrs Moody made us both a cup of tea in her office.

'I wanted to have a chat with you about Sean,' she said as we settled down. 'Over the past couple of days he's been very disruptive. He's been throwing things, pushing other children. We've had to remove him from the classroom and he's spent most of the time sitting on the floor under the table. He'd been doing so well but it's almost like we've gone back to the behaviour we saw in the first few weeks. Has anything happened at home, Maggie?'

I sighed as I nodded.

'I was about to mention this to his teacher actually,' I told her. 'The children's social worker came round last week to talk to them about looking for adoptive parents. Understandably I think it's unsettled Sean.'

'Aaah, that makes complete sense.' Mrs Moody nodded. 'So their social worker feels the children are ready to be adopted?'

'She thinks so,' I said. 'Obviously it might take a while given that there are three of them. I know Sean's having a bit of a wobble but it's still all very new so hopefully his behaviour will settle down.'

'Well, now we know what's causing it, we'll try and handle it as sensitively as we can.' She smiled.

A few days later Lisa arranged for the adoption social worker to come round and meet the children for the first time. Her name was Marie and she was tiny. Although she was small, I quickly learnt that she had a loud voice and was full of energy.

'Well, I love a challenge, and finding a family for a sibling group of three is certainly that.' She smiled as the two of us sat down on the sofa.

'Has Lisa told you much about them?' I asked in a low voice, aware of the children playing next door.

'Oh yes,' she said. 'I believe they were a bit of a handful at first but she says that you've done a great job.'

'It's very early days though,' I cautioned. 'They've just started to get settled but we still have our ups and downs.'

'Well, I think I'd better meet these three then,' she said.

I took her through to the kitchen where the children were sitting on the floor playing.

They looked up curiously as she walked in.

'Hello, I'm Marie,' she said, in a voice that sounded a like a children's TV presenter. 'I work at Social Services with Lisa.'

She went and sat down on the floor next to them.

'So you know how Lisa told you that we're going to start looking for a forever family for you?' she asked them.

Mary nodded.

'Have you found one already?' Dougie wondered, his eyes wide.

'Not just yet, I'm afraid,' she laughed. 'My job is to look through all my papers to see which mummies and daddies want to have three children to come and live with them. Have you been thinking what kind of a mummy and daddy you might like?' she asked them.

'Will you find ones that like pink cos I really like that colour?' said Mary.

'I want you to find ones that give us food like Maggie,' added Dougie.

'Don't worry, Marie will definitely make sure they have lots and lots of food in their cupboards,' I reassured him.

I could see that some of their old fears were creeping back.

Marie played with them for a little while and then they went into the front room to watch TV so the pair of us could have a chat.

'So what happens now?' I asked her.

'I'll put some feelers out and start the search,' she replied. 'I'll see if we've got any suitable couples on our books in the local authority and if we haven't then I'll put it out county-wide.

'In fact often it's preferable if children are adopted out of the area as there's no chance of them bumping into their biological parents or them being able to track them down.'

'Their biological parents are in prison,' I told her.

'Lisa did mention that.' Marie nodded. 'But a few years down the line when they come out they're likely to head back to the same area. I know Lisa says they're showing no interest in seeing the children at the minute, but you don't know what four years in prison might do to somebody.'

Marie also talked about the fact that they'd probably want to advertise the children in local newspapers and magazines. Local authorities often did that with older children or large sibling groups that were harder to place.

'Advertising kids always feels a bit odd to me,' I sighed. 'They're children, not cars or houses.'

'We'll make sure their names are changed and we'll get some nice professional photographs taken of them,' Marie told me. 'It really does work, Maggie.'

Even though I felt uncomfortable about it, if it found the children adoptive parents then who was I to argue? I had to trust Social Service's judgement on that one.

'How long will you give it?' I asked Marie.

I was painfully aware that they might not find anyone willing to take on three older, damaged children.

'If we don't find anyone within six months, we'll give up on adoption and look at long-term fostering instead,' she said.

I prayed that it wouldn't come to that. Even though it was presented in the kindest way so the children didn't blame themselves, after talking to them about forever families for months it was always such a let-down for them when one couldn't be found.

'Let's keep in touch and I'll fill you in on any updates,' promised Marie.

As the days passed, I could see Sean was still unsettled. His behaviour at school was up and down and he was very quiet and withdrawn.

One morning I decided to have a clear-out of the toy cupboard. There were still quite a few toddler toys in there from a previous placement and I wanted to make room for a few board games that I had in the loft and thought the children might enjoy.

However, as I opened the cupboard doors, a horrific stench hit my nostrils.

Not again, I thought to myself.

I breathed in through my mouth as I sorted through the toys and tried to find the cause of the problem. Eventually I discovered it – I took the lid off a Lego box and almost gagged as I saw the pile of faeces inside it.

'Oh, Sean,' I sighed to myself. 'Poor lad.'

It wasn't pleasant to deal with, but I understood why he'd done it. When children are feeling worried or insecure they will often regress to their old ways. This was Sean's way of showing his anxiety about being adopted.

I got out my rubber gloves and by the time I'd picked the children up from school and brought them home, the house smelt of bleach and the Lego box and bricks were on their second cycle in the dishwasher.

Later in the week Marie phoned to say she'd arranged for a photographer to come round to the house to take some pictures of the children.

'Marie would like to get some nice photographs of you so she can show them to your forever mummy and daddy when she finds them,' I explained.

'But you've got loads of pictures of us on your phone,' said Mary, looking confused.

'Yes, but these will be really special ones,' I told her. 'Marie has arranged for a special person called a photographer to come round here. He'll have a big camera and lots of lights and before he comes we're going to go shopping so you have something new to wear.'

That weekend we went shopping and Mary picked out a velvet dress with a sparkly collar and I got matching navy blue cords and stripy shirts for the boys.

The photographer was a friendly man called Julian who was in his fifties. He was really patient with the children and he showed them his camera and let them help him set up the backdrop and the lights in the kitchen. Even Sean watched curiously as he set up all his equipment.

He made the whole experience really fun for them.

'I don't do boring sitting-down photos,' he explained, smiling at the children.

He got them doing forward rolls, pulling silly faces and all leaping in the air at the same time. It was lovely to see Sean having fun and messing about with his brother and sister like other children.

'I've got some great shots.' Julian grinned at me as he packed up, looking pleased.

I hoped they would be enough to help find the children their new mummy and daddy.

As the weeks passed, there were no new developments. Whenever Lisa came round, Dougie and Mary would leap on her and ask: 'Have you found us a forever family yet?'

'Not yet,' Lisa would tell them. 'Marie is still looking very, very hard.'

Sean would always be hovering around in the background listening in.

I was in regular touch with Marie and she kept me updated on her search.

'Unfortunately there's no one suitable in this area so we're going to start looking out of the county,' she explained after a month of no news.

The breakthrough came nearly two months after that when Marie called me one morning just after I'd dropped the children at school. They'd been with me for eight months by this point.

'Maggie, I'm going out to see a couple this week and I'd love to take them a little video clip of the kids,' she said. 'Do you think you could take one tonight and email it to me?'

My heart started thumping.

'What, you've found someone?' I gabbled. 'Have they said they want to adopt them?'

'No, not yet,' she told me. 'But I've got a good feeling about them so I'm hopeful.'

Marie didn't want to tell me much at this stage except for the fact that she had been out to see them once and they wanted to know more about the children.

'Don't get your hopes up,' she warned me. 'I'll keep you posted.'

That afternoon after school, as the children played a game of Snakes and Ladders, I recorded a little clip of them on my phone. I wanted it to be real and not staged but at the same time I wasn't going to send them one of them rolling around the floor having a tantrum. I wanted them to see the children as they were.

'Maggie, why are you taking a photo?' asked Mary.

'Because you're playing so nicely.' I smiled.

'Do you think our new mummy and daddy will like to play Snakes and Ladders?' asked Dougie.

'I hope so,' I said. 'And if they don't then you'll have to teach them.'

Over the next few days I tried to put it out of my mind but later that week Marie's number flashed up on my phone.

'Well? I asked her. 'How did it go?'

'Great news, Maggie,' she said. 'I think we've found our adopters.'

ELEVEN

A Family Found

A mixture of nerves, worry and delight filled my body as Marie described the couple that wanted to adopt the children.

Their names were Gillian and Adrian McKenna.

'He's got a lovely Scottish accent although they don't live there now,' explained Marie. 'They're based in a town a couple of hours away from here.'

I listened as she told me all about them. Adrian was an accountant and Gillian was a nurse and both of them were in their mid-forties. He had been married before and had two grown-up children. They'd got married five years ago but had been unable to have children of their own.

'Gillian wants to give up work to be a stay-at-home mum when they adopt the kids, which is admirable,' said Marie.

'They've got a lovely house, Maggie. A three-bed new build, nice big garden and it was absolutely immaculate. I think they're perfect and they're delighted to take on all three of them – a ready-made family, as Gillian calls it. Adrian wasn't that keen on adopting a baby or a toddler as he's been through that before so they're both very excited by the idea of three older children.'

I'd had my doubts that there was someone out there who was willing to take on these three damaged children, but it seemed as though Marie had proved me wrong.

'It sounds like on paper they tick every box,' I said.

I was comforted by the fact Gillian was a nurse as in my experience nurses tended to be kind, patient people.

'They'll go in front of a matching panel in two weeks,' said Marie. 'In the meantime have you got some recent photos of the children that I can take with me when I next go and see them?'

'They've got the professional ones, but I thought it would be nice to take some others to show them. Maybe some more informal, everyday ones.'

'Yes of course,' I replied. 'I'll dig some out on my phone and email them over to you.'

'Obviously we can't say anything to the children or anyone else until they've been approved by the matching panel, but it all looks good to me,' said Marie.

'That's brilliant,' I sighed. 'I'm so pleased and relieved.'

I genuinely was. After talking to them about forever families for the past three months, as time had passed, I had become more and more aware of their impending sense of impatience and disappointment when Marie or Lisa had said they hadn't got any news. Of course mixed in with delight for the children was a growing sense of sadness as I knew they would soon be leaving me.

It was so hard not being able to share the news with the children when they got home from school that afternoon. I was bursting with excitement and it was frustrating not being able to say anything to them. It's a strange feeling to have this life-changing information but not be able to share it with anyone – neither the children nor Louisa.

'How was school?' I asked Sean, who was sketching his favourite butterflies at the kitchen table.

He didn't reply and looked downcast. He was still struggling and I wondered how he was going to take the news that they were going to be adopted. I knew that Mary and Dougie would be excited but he'd been so down about it.

The following morning I bumped into Carol on the way back from the school run.

'Do you fancy coming in for a cuppa?' I asked her.

She still provided the odd bit of respite care for me if I needed to go to a meeting or training and couldn't be back in time for school pick-up. We got on well and I knew that as a fellow foster carer, I could talk to her about the adopters and she would keep it confidential.

'Obviously keep this to yourself, but it looks like they've found a couple to adopt the children,' I told her.

'What?' she gasped, putting her cup down. 'That's great news.'

However, the look on her face told me something different.

'You seem a bit disappointed,' I said, puzzled. 'Aren't you pleased?'

'Of course I'm pleased, Maggie,' she sighed. 'I'll just be sad to see them go. I've grown fond of all three of them, especially Sean.'

'Really?' I asked, curious as to why she felt an affinity with the child who was the most troubled. 'Why Sean?'

'He's just so vulnerable,' she explained. 'And he's such a sweet boy at times when you catch him on his own.'

'You're right,' I sighed. 'My big worry is how he's going to take this adoption news.'

'How are you feeling about it all?' asked Carol. 'I know how attached you are to the children.'

'It doesn't really feel real at the moment,' I sighed. 'I don't think it will until this couple has been approved at panel and we all meet them.'

The fortnight leading up to the matching panel seemed to go painfully slowly. Normally it was a foregone conclusion that the matching panel would agree with Social Service's decision that the couple were a good match for the children, but it was never 100 per cent definite. Meanwhile at home I kept up the conversations about forever families.

'I wonder if Marie has managed to find you a forever mummy and daddy yet?' I said aloud the next evening as I cooked dinner.

'She's been looking for a long, long time,' sighed Mary. 'I think she should have found us one by now.'

'Me too,' agreed Dougie.

'Well, I'm going to give her a ring tomorrow and ask her,' I told them. 'What do you think, Sean?'

He just shrugged.

Marie phoned me the day before Adrian and Gillian were due to meet the panel.

'They're going in front of the panel in the morning,' she said. 'So all being well, how about we meet you tomorrow afternoon at 2 p.m. at Social Services?'

'Great,' I said. 'I'll get Carol to pick the children up from school and bring them back here for dinner.'

'If you don't hear from me, Maggie, then assume everything has gone well and I'll see you tomorrow,' Marie told me.

'Finger crossed,' I said.

'It will be fine,' she soothed. 'I'm sure it will. Honestly, they're perfect, Maggie.'

Even though I'd never met them I felt nervous on Adrian and Gillian's behalf. All the next morning I had butterflies in my stomach as I kept myself busy sorting out paperwork and doing some cleaning. For once in my life I was willing my phone not to ring.

By the time Carol came round after lunch, I was a bag of nerves.

'Have you heard yet?' she asked. 'Did they pass their panel?'

'Marie said she'd only call if there was a problem,' I told her. 'So I'm going to assume that it has all gone OK.'

As I drove to the Social Services building in town, I felt nervous. I was meeting the couple that wanted to adopt these children who I'd invested a huge amount of time, energy and love on and I so desperately wanted it to be right for them. There was so much riding on this and after everything they'd been through, Dougie, Mary and Sean deserved to have a happy ending with a family that would love and care for them.

I was curious to find out what Gillian and Adrian were like, too. Over the next few weeks they'd be coming into my home and I was going to be spending a lot of time with them so it was important that I got on with them.

As I walked into Social Services reception, I tried to put all my worries to the back of my mind. Marie was waiting for me there, along with Becky who was also coming along to the meeting.

'Maggie, you look so worried.' She smiled. 'There's no need. It all went fine and they passed their panel with flying colours.'

'Thank God for that,' I sighed.

'As you can imagine, Adrian and Gillian are ecstatic. They're very much looking forward to meeting you.'

'And me them.' I grinned.

'They're just in the office down here with Lisa,' said Marie, and we followed her down a long corridor. The door was open and a couple was sitting around the small table. They jumped up as we came in and looked expectantly at Becky and me, obviously unsure of who was who.

'This is Adrian and Gillian,' said Marie.

Adrian was extremely tall and slight. He had greying short hair and he looked like he'd come from the office in a suit, shirt and tie. Gillian was very smartly dressed too in a black trouser suit and blouse. She had long auburn hair tied back in a ponytail. They both wore similar wire-framed glasses that made them look rather studious and bookish. I was struck by how serious they both looked, but I reasoned that they were probably both exhausted after the stress of the panel.

I held out my hand to Gillian and she shook it.

'I'm Maggie.' I smiled. 'The children's foster carer.'

I noticed that she wasn't wearing any jewellery except for a simple gold wedding band and there was no nail varnish on her short nails

'Ah, you're the famous Maggie,' she said with a wry smile. 'The miracle worker!'

'Oh I'm not a miracle worker, I can assure you of that,' I told her, laughing nervously. I wasn't sure if she was being sarcastic or not.

'Congratulations to you both, you must be very excited.' I smiled at Adrian as I shook his hand.

'Yes, we're very happy.' He nodded. 'We've wanted a family for a long time.'

'Well, I'm full of admiration for anyone willing to take on a large sibling group,' said Becky as Marie introduced her to them.

'It's an ideal combination in my book,' Gillian told her, matter-of-factly. 'An older girl and two younger boys. A ready-made family.'

Marie got us all a drink as we settled around the table.

'How has it been fostering the children?' asked Gillian, as soon as we'd sat down.

I hesitated.

When I meet parents who are about to adopt children, I don't pull any punches. My belief is they need to know their full history, warts and all, and we'd be doing them a disservice if they didn't. In my view it was very important that parents went into an adoption with their eyes well and truly open.

'I'm going to be honest with you,' I told them. 'The first few weeks with them were hell. They were literally running wild as I'm sure Marie has told you. It was impossible to do even basic things with the boys like give them a bath or get them dressed. I had to physically catch them on a morning and resort to giving them ice pops to keep them still and to try and calm them.'

I saw Gillian's face drop.

'Isn't that considered as bribery or rewarding bad behaviour?' she asked sternly, her brow furrowed.

'It's actually a proven technique for children who have been through trauma,' Becky said, jumping in. 'Ice pops or ice cream or even lollipops can be really effective in getting children to calm down.'

Even as I went on to explain the theory behind it, Gillian still looked shocked.

'Well, I don't think we'll be giving them lollies for breakfast at our house, will we, Adrian?' She smiled.

'You'll be seeing a lot more of Maggie but is there anything you'd like to know about the children now?' Marie asked them, clearly trying to steer the conversation back on course.

'We heard that you had a big struggle getting the children to use the toilet when they first came to live with you,' said Adrian. 'So are they fully toilet-trained now?'

'Yes, the first few weeks were fun,' I said. 'They're OK now but often when the boys have wobbles or they're stressed or upset they can go back to their old ways and soil themselves, especially Sean. But put it this way, it's less often that I'm finding poo behind the curtains or in the toy box any more.'

Out of the corner of my eye I noticed Gillian flinch.

'Gosh, I don't know how you deal with that.' She grimaced.

'You get used to it,' I reassured her. 'In fact it doesn't bother me any more.

'Marie mentioned that you're a nurse so you must be used to dealing with bodily functions too?'

'Actually, I'm a matron,' she said huffily, 'So my role largely involves managing people and wards now.'

I could see that she was a little put out that I had thought that she was a nurse.

'What sort of things do the children like doing?' asked Adrian.

'Well Sean is really into his Lego,' I said. 'Dougie loves building with the wooden train track and Mary loves playing simple card games like Snap and messing about with people's hair.'

'What about swimming?' asked Gillian. 'We really enjoy it and I think it's so important that children know how to swim. Have they had lessons?'

'I haven't taken them swimming yet,' I replied. 'It's only recently because of their behaviour that I've been able to take them to any public places. For the first three months or so I generally kept everything home-based because that's all they could cope with.'

'What about cycling?' Adrian continued. 'That's something else we both enjoy.'

'Again it's not something we've had chance to do yet. I'm assuming the children don't know how to ride a bike so perhaps that something you can all do together in the future?'

'Have you got any pets?' I asked them, knowing how all three children had said they wanted a mummy and a daddy with a dog.

'Oh no,' said Gillian, shaking her head. 'We're not what you'd call animal people. And they make too much of a mess for my liking.'

And so do three children, I thought to myself, a flicker of doubt crossing my mind.

Mary had gradually learnt to be tidier but the boys were still another matter.

'We noticed from the photos that Marie gave us that Sean's got very long hair,' Gillian went on. 'Has he not been to the hairdressers?'

'He has.' I nodded. 'However, while Dougie was happy to have his cut, Sean was very nervous and he said he wanted to keep his long. Their hair is so lovely now compared to the matted, dirty dreadlocks they had when they first arrived.'

'Oh I think short hair looks so much nicer on boys,' Gillian told me. 'Don't you, Adrian?'

'Yes, we don't want anyone mistaking him for a girl, do we?' He smiled.

The conversation quickly turned to how we were going to break the news to Mary, Sean and Dougie.

'So when are you going to tell them?' I asked.

'Well if it's OK with you I could come back today and talk to them?' suggested Lisa. 'I could drive back and meet you at your house.'

'I don't see why not,' I told her. 'Strike while the iron's hot.'

'That means that Adrian and Gillian could possibly come round a couple of days later and meet the children?' suggested Marie.

'Yes,' I agreed. 'Friday after school would be good and that gives them a couple of days to get used to the idea.'

I noticed Adrian squeeze Gillian's hand.

'Oh I can't wait to see them.' She smiled.

It was a relief to see their excitement about meeting the children and I felt guilty that maybe I'd judged them too harshly. I knew how stressful and exhausting it was going in front of a panel and it had been a long day for them.

Becky and I said our goodbyes and left, leaving Gillian and Adrian to sort out some paperwork with Marie.

'I'll be five minutes behind you, Maggie,' Lisa called out. 'See you at your house.'

As the lift doors closed, Becky turned to me.

'So what did you think of them?' she asked.

'They seem nice.' I shrugged. 'It's very difficult to get a true picture of people when you initially meet them and they've had the stress and anxiety of going to panel this morning.'

'Maggie, I've known you long enough for you to tell me what you really think,' Becky laughed.

'Well, they seemed a little bit brusque to me. They weren't very warm and all their questions were about cleanliness and hygiene, or else telling us about what *they* enjoyed, which I thought was a bit odd,' I told her. 'I'm probably taking this personally but I got the sense that they disapproved of me somehow.'

'Well that doesn't matter, even if it is the case,' Becky assured me. 'It's the children they're adopting, not you.'

'I know.' I smiled. 'I'm probably being oversensitive and picky. Let's put it down to nerves.'

'I'm sure that once they meet the children and have been round to the house and seen what a brilliant job you've done with them, they'll relax,' Becky said.

'You're probably right,' I agreed.

It's hard to get the true measure of people in such a short space of time and I was probably judging them too harshly.

I pulled up outside the house and was just looking for my keys when Lisa drove in behind me.

'That was quick,' I laughed.

'Let's go and do this.' She smiled.

My heart was in my mouth as I opened the front door.

They were all sitting round the kitchen table, laughing at something Dougie had just said. I felt a rush of pride as I looked at them, and I was struck yet again by how different they were from the wild creatures that had arrived at my door a few months previously.

'They've just finished their tea and they're having some fruit and a yogurt,' said Carol, who was washing up some plates.

'Look who I've brought to see you.' I smiled. 'Lisa's come round because she's got some very exciting news to tell you.'

They looked at her expectantly as they licked their spoons.

'Do you want me to go?' asked Carol, drying her hands on a tea towel.

'No, you can stay and hear the good news,' Lisa told her.

'What is it?' demanded Mary, her eyes wide.

'Remember Lisa told you how she and Marie were going to look very hard to find you a forever mummy and daddy?' I told them. 'Well she's been out to see lots and lots of different ones and guess what? She's found a mummy and daddy who really want you to live with them. I met them this afternoon and they're absolutely lovely.'

Mary and Dougie started jumping around with excitement.

'What, they really want us?' asked Mary, her eyes shiny with excitement.

'They really want all three of you.' Lisa smiled. 'They're going to come round and meet you in a couple of days but in the meantime they've sent you a special book to have a look at so you can find out all about them.'

'Can I see it first?' yelled Dougie.

'No, I want it!' giggled Mary.

'Let's open it up on the table and we can all look at it together,' I added.

Dougie and Mary crowded round me as I opened the photo album. Sean carried on eating his yogurt, carefully scraping every last bit out of the pot with his spoon.

'Sean, are you coming to look at it?' I asked him.

'No,' he grunted. 'F**k off.'

I decided not to force the issue. I wanted him to look at it in his own time when he was ready. I opened up the book and on the first page was a photo of Adrian and Gillian. They were both smiling but they were standing stiffly in their front driveway. Carol and Lisa oohed and aahed at the photos.

'Look, that's your forever mummy and daddy.' Lisa smiled. 'Aren't they lovely?'

Hello children, our names are Adrian and Gillian, they'd written underneath the picture.

Mary read out the words carefully, and then began chattering excitedly.

'Oh look, Gillian's got a ponytail,' she exclaimed. 'I put my hair in a ponytail, don't I, Maggie?

'Can I have a ponytail, in my hair tomorrow when I go to school so I look like Gillian? Has she got earrings?'

'I don't think so, sweetie,' I said.

I'd got Lisa to make three photocopies of that first photo so each child had their own picture of their new parents.

'Lisa has got a photo of your forever mummy and daddy for each of you so you can look at them in your own time later on,' I told them. 'Shall we have a flick through the rest of the book?'

Sean was still ignoring what was going on and was playing with a pile of Connect Four counters that were lying on the table. But as we flicked through the book, I noticed him giving little sideways glances at the photos. However, I didn't say anything to him or try and involve him in the conversation. I didn't want to force him to look and I wanted him to absorb it all in his own time.

The next photo was of the outside of Adrian and Gillian's house – a neat brick detached. The other photos were of the living room, the garden and what was going to be Sean and Dougie's bedroom and then Mary's. They were all painted cream.

'What lovely bedrooms,' I enthused as Dougie and Mary tried to take it all in.

When we got to the end, Dougie looked upset.

'But there wasn't a dog, Maggie,' he cried, his blue eyes shining with tears.

'Well, they've got an amazing swing in the garden,' I soothed. 'You'll like that, won't you?'

'When will we see our new mummy and daddy?' asked Dougie.

'I'm going to call them Adrian and Gillian,' said Mary firmly.

'Marie and I are going to bring them round to meet you after school on Friday,' Lisa told them. 'Is that OK?'

Dougie and Mary nodded excitedly but Sean showed no reaction and stared distractedly out of the window.

I found the children some Blu Tack.

'I thought you might want to stick the photo of your forever family on your bedroom wall,' I suggested. 'You can put them wherever you want.'

Mary and Dougie took one each and rushed off.

I went over and handed a photo to Sean.

'Don't want it,' he muttered.

'Take it upstairs, lovey, in case you want to look at it later.'

He snatched it off me and stomped off upstairs with the other two.

'Well I think that went OK,' said Lisa.

'I suppose so,' I sighed. 'Sean's the one that concerns me.'

'He'll come round in time,' Lisa reassured me.

I hoped she was right. After I'd said goodbye to her I went upstairs to see how the children were getting on.

'Maggie look, I've put my photo up,' exclaimed Mary, eagerly showing me how she'd stuck hers on the wardrobe.

'Come and see mine,' shouted Dougie.

I went into his bedroom to see his stuck on the side of his bedside table.

'I put my new mummy and daddy there so I can see them when I'm in bed.' He smiled.

'That's a great idea,' I told him.

Sean had already gone back downstairs.

'Where's Sean put his?' I asked Dougie and he shrugged.

It was only when I was tidying up later and I bent down to pick something up off the floor that I saw something stuffed under Sean's bed.

It was a crumpled sheet of paper, screwed up in a ball.

I opened it and my heart sank. It was the photo of Gillian and Adrian and he'd scribbled in black pen all over their faces.

I wanted to believe that Lisa was right and in time Sean was going to get used to the idea of moving on and being adopted but after his reaction this afternoon, I wasn't so sure. For the adoption to go ahead, all three children needed to be fully on board.

TWELVE

The First Meeting

That night, after I'd put the children to bed, Marie rang me.

'Lisa said telling the children went well,' she gushed.

'Yes it was OK,' I replied, keen not to dress it up. 'Sean wasn't willing to engage at all, but Dougie and Mary are excited. I'm hoping that in time he'll come round to the idea.'

'And what did you think of Adrian and Gillian?' she asked. 'They're great, aren't they? I think the children are going to love them.'

I hesitated. 'Yes, they seemed very nice,' I said.

She must have sensed I was a little bit unsure because she added: 'I know they might have come across as a little anxious but I'm sure they'll be a lot more relaxed when they meet the kids. They're a slightly older couple and they're not used to dealing with young children so I think it's just a bit daunting for them.'

Marie sounded so positive and enthusiastic that I felt guilty for not instantly warming to them.

In all honesty, I was dreading Friday when Adrian and Gillian met the children for the first time. There was so much riding on it and I really wanted it to go well, but I had no idea how the children were going to react, particularly Sean. I knew what they were like when they'd first met me. None of them coped well with change and despite Mary and Dougie's initial excitement, I couldn't help but worry that their old insecurities would come out and their behaviour would deteriorate.

The next morning when I took the children to school, I told their teachers the news about their adoption and I left the book of photos with the office so they could each take it in turns to show it to their class. It was important that everyone got involved in their adoption and was enthusiastic about it.

But when I went to collect it that afternoon, Angela, the school secretary, pulled me to one side.

'I'm afraid Sean wasn't too keen on showing it to his class,' she told me. 'Mary and Dougie had it this morning so I took it into his classroom this afternoon but he wasn't happy, Maggie. He got very angry and upset and his teacher said it would be best if I took it back to the office.'

'I'm really sorry about that,' I sighed. 'But thanks for letting me know.'

It made me even more anxious about him meeting Adrian and Gillian the following day. I knew that Sean had a strong sense of loyalty to his brother and sister so all I could hope was that if he saw Mary and Dougie reacting well to them then he would accept them too.

On the way home from school that afternoon we called into the supermarket.

'Why are we coming here?' asked Sean sulkily.

'We're going to buy some cakes so that when you meet your forever family tomorrow we can all have a little tea party.'

I'd realised by this point that calling them Mummy and Daddy in front of Sean was a bit of a trigger. My thoughts were that if there was food involved, then they would sit nicely and it might help calm Sean.

Sean dragged his feet up and down the cake aisle.

'Don't like those,' he spat at everything I suggested.

'What about these?' I asked, picking up some plain fairy cakes.

'They're s**t,' he complained.

'Well I seem to remember last time I bought these, you ate every last one of them so they can't be that bad,' I told him and at last he gave me a wry smile. I realised it was the first time I'd seen him smile since he'd learnt about the adoption.

We bought the cakes and Mary and Dougie chose some tubes of coloured icing to decorate them with.

That evening I got them to bed as early as possible so that they all had a good night's sleep. The following morning I woke up with my stomach churning, worrying about how the meeting was going to go.

As I made everyone breakfast, Louisa obviously sensed my nerves. She had been delighted when I told her that adoptive parents had been found.

'Is it today they're going to meet their new mum and dad?' she asked me quietly.

I nodded.

'Oh, Maggie, don't look so worried,' she reassured me. 'I'm sure it's going to be fine.'

'I really hope so,' I sighed.

Before she left for work, Louisa sat down at the table with the children and chatted to them.

'You're meeting your new forever family tonight, aren't you?' she asked conversationally, and Mary and Dougie nodded enthusiastically.

'Yeah, they're coming round for a tea party,' Dougie squealed, bouncing up and down in his chair.

'That sounds lovely,' Louisa replied kindly. 'I wish I was coming. I'm staying at Charlie's tonight but when I get back tomorrow, will you promise me that you'll tell me all about it?'

'We promise.' Mary smiled.

All day I had a sick feeling in the pit of my stomach that wouldn't go away. The house was spotless by the time I went to pick the children up from school. Mary and Dougie were as high as kites while Sean was sullen-faced.

'When are they going to be here?' asked Mary the second we got home, twirling around the kitchen with excitement.

'I'm not sure,' I told her. 'They said they were going to pop in for a cup of tea after school with Marie and Lisa.'

I rummaged in the cupboard and got out the cakes and the tubes of icing that we'd bought the previous day.

'Now I've got a very important job for you all,' I told them. 'You need to ice the first letter of everyone's names on the top of their cake.'

I wanted to give them an activity to do to occupy them and calm their nerves before everyone arrived. Also it was nice to get them doing something for their forever family and remind them who was coming.

'So who's going to do your new mummy's cake and who's going to do your new daddy's?' I asked them.

'I ain't doing none of them.' Sean glared.

'That's OK, lovey, you can just watch,' I told him cheerfully.

'I'll do one for the daddy,' said Dougie eagerly.

I watched as he carefully iced a wobbly 'D' on one of the cakes.

'I'll do the one for Gillian,' said Mary.

I noticed that she'd done a 'J' rather than 'G' but she'd taken such care over it that I didn't have the heart to point out her mistake.

She was just finishing it off when the doorbell rang. My heart was in my mouth as I went to answer it. Marie and Lisa were standing there with a very nervous-looking Adrian and Gillian. Adrian wasn't wearing a suit this time but was still dressed very smartly in a shirt and trousers, and Gillian had on a blouse and a skirt. I suddenly felt very scruffy in my jeans, jumper and fluffy slippers.

'Come on in.' I smiled. 'The children are in the kitchen.'

They all looked up as we walked in.

'Hello, kids, how are you?' Marie greeted them. 'This is Adrian and this is Gillian. And they're so excited to meet you.'

They both looked extremely unsure and uncomfortable as the children stared at them.

'Why don't you go over and say hello,' Marie urged them gently.

They walked over to the table where the kids were sitting.

'Hello, you must be Dougie,' said Adrian formally, holding out his hand so Dougie could shake it.

Dougie stared at it, unsure of what to do. My heart went out to him, knowing he'd never shaken anyone's hand before.

'Hello,' Dougie replied in a very serious voice, after finally taking Adrian's outstretched hand to hold in his own. 'Have you got a dog at your house?'

'Um, no, I'm afraid we haven't,' replied Adrian, looking taken aback.

'Right then, shall I make everyone a hot drink?' I said loudly in a desperate attempt to break the ice.

Lisa stepped in to help with the introductions while I busied myself with putting the kettle on.

'Mary, do you want to give everyone the cakes that we made?' I asked her.

'You're lying,' growled Sean who up until now had been sitting at the table and glowering as the scene unfolded. 'We didn't make them.'

'Well, Sean's right,' I said. 'I suppose we did cheat a little bit as we didn't make the cakes from scratch but the children iced them themselves especially.'

Poor Gillian and Adrian still looked terribly uncomfortable and weren't sure where to put themselves.

'Sit down and make yourselves at home,' I told them. 'Mary will get you both a cake.'

Mary, bless her, got to work.

'Oh wow, have you made one for me as well?' asked Marie when Mary offered up hers. 'That's very kind of you. I love cakes.'

'Which one's mine?' asked Gillian with a confused look on her face.

'It's this one,' Mary pointed. 'I did yours,' she added proudly.

'Oh dear, it's a "J" when it should be a "G",' she sighed. 'Never mind. I'm sure it will still taste delicious,' she added quickly, but I saw the look of disappointment flash across Mary's little face. She'd tried so hard to make it perfect and I felt heartbroken for her.

By the time I'd brought the drinks over, the atmosphere was still very stilted. The children clearly didn't know what to say so they sat in a row with their heads down, eating their cakes in silence while the adults continued making polite conversation.

'We loved your photo book, Adrian and Gillian,' I spoke up brightly. 'Didn't we, kids? Your house looks so exciting. Mary, can you remember what colour the front door was?'

'Blue?' she asked uncertainly.

Gillian shook her head.

'Red?' guessed Dougie.

'Sean, can you remember?' I asked him, smiling encouragingly.

'No,' he snapped, shoving the last bit of cake into his mouth.

'It's black actually,' said Gillian.

I cast around for something to say to fill the awkward silence.

'Dougie, why don't you go and get our photo album from the front room then Adrian and Gillian can see what you've all been doing here?'

I thought it would be a good way to encourage conversation and get them interacting with each other. I glanced nervously over at Sean who'd got up from the table and was now kicking a football against the patio doors, his whole body tensed.

'Can we have tea now, Maggie?' he yelled. 'I'm hungry. I want tea now.'

'Not yet, Sean,' I told him calmly. 'You've just had a cake and it's too early.'

Gillian and Adrian shifted uncomfortably in their seats, obviously unsure what to make of this outburst.

Dougie came running back with the photo album outstretched, and he and Mary gathered round as I opened it up on the table. Gillian flicked through it quickly before stopping abruptly at one of the photos, a look of horror on her face. I glanced over her shoulder to see a picture of the kids sitting at the kitchen table, beaming up at the camera, their faces absolutely covered in chocolate mousse.

Mary started giggling.

'That was the time we didn't use spoons to eat our mousse and we just licked it out of the pot with our tongues.'

'Yeah,' laughed Dougie. 'That was good, that was.'

'You used your tongues?' questioned Gillian in a disapproving tone, clearly not impressed.

'It was part of the process of teaching the children about food,' I explained, noticing how Dougie and Mary's faces had fallen. 'We were exploring different textures and learning that food can be both delicious and fun.'

Gillian continued to stare at the picture disapprovingly, as though she was scared that some of the mess would transfer from the picture onto her crisp blouse.

'But what do we use now to eat chocolate mousse?' I asked Mary and Dougie brightly.

'Spoons!' they both chorused.

Lisa and Marie laughed, but Gillian and Adrian didn't crack a smile.

Sensing the tension in the room, I quickly changed the subject.

'Dougie and Sean, why don't you take Adrian upstairs and show him your bedroom, and, Mary, do you want to show Gillian yours?'

'I'm not showing him nothing,' spat Sean.

'Well I'm sure Dougie can manage on his own then.' I smiled, trying to diffuse Sean's hostility.

'Come on then.' Dougie grinned at Adrian, grabbing his hand and pulling him out of the room.

Sean went stomping after them.

'Well I'm coming too cos it's my bedroom as well,' he huffed.

Gillian and Mary followed closely behind, Mary glancing up at Gillian every now and again, a look of awe on her face.

I got up and started clearing away the cups and plates.

'You're right, Maggie, Sean doesn't seem very keen at all,' sighed Lisa, once the footsteps had retreated upstairs.

'Actually, things are going a lot better than I expected,' I told them honestly. 'There haven't been any massive melt-downs or arguments.'

Sean had always seemed the most damaged child of the three and I knew he wasn't going to immediately embrace Adrian and Gillian and start calling them Mummy and Daddy. Neither was Mary for that matter. They were older children and what had happened with their biological parents had taught them never to trust adults. Why should they trust these two strangers?

It was going to take time for all three of them to adjust and get to know this couple.

'Maggie, are you OK if Marie and I leave you to it?' asked Lisa.

'Yes of course.' I nodded.

'Try and keep their visit to no longer than an hour and a half,' advised Marie. 'Otherwise it will be too much for everyone. I've already had a word with Gillian and Adrian and said the same thing.'

'No problem,' I replied, meaning it.

I already felt exhausted, so I could only imagine how the children felt.

Once I'd seen Lisa and Marie out, I went upstairs to see how they were getting on. Dougie had pulled out half of his toy cupboard and was showing Adrian some of his favourites while Sean was lying face down on his bed, silent and unmoving.

'Boys, how about you choose a soft toy to give to Adrian, then he can take it back to your new house so when you go round it will be there waiting for you?' I suggested.

'That's a great idea.' Adrian smiled.

'I'll give him Ted,' Dougie exclaimed, hurrying to pick up the little brown bear from his bed.

'I'm not giving that man nothing,' scowled Sean.

I left Dougie chattering excitedly to Adrian about his favourite toys and popped my head around Mary's bedroom door to see her talking Gillian through her extensive collection of cuddly toys.

'These are called Beany Boos and I love them,' she explained, cuddling the little toys and I smiled to see her little face looking so animated.

'Over the next few days I'll get the children to gradually pack up their things so you can start to take them back,' I told Gillian.

'I'm going to bring all my cuddlies,' stated Mary.

'Well you've only got a small bedroom,' Gillian told her. 'You might want to leave some of them here with Maggie.'

Mary's face crumpled and she looked horrified.

'I'm taking all my cuddlies,' she wailed, clutching a handful of them to her chest dramatically.

'In her own house she didn't have anything of her own, so she hangs onto things more than most children would,' I explained quietly to Gillian. 'Her soft toys are really important to her.'

'You love them to bits, don't you, sweetie?' I said to Mary, and she nodded, her eyes wide.

'She can name every single one of them.' I laughed. 'In fact, every night when I put Mary to bed, I have to say goodnight to a long line of teddies too.'

'You can do it too if you want, when I come to live at your house,' Mary told Gillian shyly.

Gillian went and sat on the bed beside Mary as she held one of her toys out to her.

'This one's my favourite,' Mary told her proudly.

Gillian looked decidedly out of her comfort zone.

'Hello, horse,' she said stiffly, patting it on the top of its head. 'It's nice to meet you.'

Mary burst out laughing.

'That's not a horse,' she giggled. 'That's Sparkle the unicorn.'

'Oh OK,' Gillian blushed, looking flustered. 'How very nice to meet you, Sparkle.'

I felt a bit sorry for her. I could tell she was doing her best, but it was clear that she wasn't used to playing with children.

'I'll go and get the boys and how about we all go back downstairs?' I suggested, relieving Gillian from meeting all of Mary's Beany Boos.

When we were back in the kitchen I encouraged Sean and Dougie to get out the Lego.

'Don't want to,' snapped Sean.

He sat in the corner sulking, but Dougie happily got out the box of bricks and he and Adrian started building a pirate ship together while Sean watched them out of the corner of his eye.

'Shall I show you one of my school reading books?' Mary asked Gillian shyly.

'Yes.' Gillian smiled, looking genuinely pleased. 'That would be lovely.'

They sat on the sofa together and Mary started reading her some of her Biff and Chip book.

This is more like it, I thought to myself, letting out a sigh of relief.

Now that everyone seemed a bit more relaxed, I busied myself with making tea. In the background I could hear Mary struggling with a few words as she read the book aloud to Gillian.

'Gosh, Mary, you're eight aren't you?' asked Gillian sternly. 'Shouldn't you know these words by now?'

I looked around, shocked, and saw that Mary had gone bright red, her blue eyes filling with tears.

I couldn't stop myself from saying something.

'Mary only started reading when she came to live with us. She's doing so well, don't you think, Gillian?'

'Oh I'm so sorry, I forgot,' she apologised to Mary. 'Yes, you are doing very well.'

Mary gave her a weak smile, but it was clear that the comment had upset her, and I couldn't help but feel a flicker of annoyance towards Gillian.

Dougie suddenly let out a huge yawn, rubbing his eyes as he fiddled with the Lego blocks. I looked at the clock and was shocked to realise that nearly an hour and a half had gone by already. The afternoon had been emotionally draining for everyone, and I suspected the children were getting tired and hungry.

'Right then, kids, dinner's going to be ready in about five minutes so we need to clear up the toys and say goodbye to Adrian and Gillian now,' I told them brightly.

'Oh OK,' said Adrian, jumping up quickly.

'Come on, darling,' he called to Gillian and she hurriedly got up off the sofa, smoothing an imaginary crease from her skirt.

'Bye then,' she called stiffly to the children, but none of them seemed very interested. Sean didn't say a word and Mary glanced up only briefly from her book.

'Bye,' she waved, before settling back down to read.

Only Dougie seemed bothered they were leaving.

'Please stay and help me build my Lego,' he begged Adrian.

'Adrian will be coming back again tomorrow so how about we put your Lego safely on a shelf and you can carry on building it with him then?' I suggested.

'I'll do it,' said Sean, running over. 'I'll put it on the shelf.'

He snatched the model off Adrian and it fell on the floor and shattered into pieces.

'You've ruined it, Sean,' yelled Dougie, bursting into tears.

Adrian and Gillian looked uncomfortable and clearly didn't know what to do.

'Don't worry, lovey, we can rebuild it,' I soothed. 'I'm sure Adrian will help you do a new one tomorrow.'

'Yes of course I will,' said Adrian kindly.

'I think everyone's tired,' I told them apologetically. 'But we'll look forward to seeing you tomorrow.'

'Thanks, Maggie.' Adrian smiled tightly. I sensed that he was relieved to be leaving.

'Yes, we'll see you then,' said Gillian dismissively, hurrying out to the hall.

As I closed the door behind them I suddenly felt exhausted too, but I had dinner and bedtime to get through first.

Taking a deep breath, I went back into the kitchen to serve up dinner, smiling brightly.

'So what did you think about your forever mummy and daddy?' I asked the children as we tucked into our fish fingers.

'I hate them,' growled Sean.

'Give them a chance, lovey,' I told him gently. 'It takes time to get to know people and you've only just met Gillian and Adrian.'

'Dougie, what did you think?'

He hesitated.

'I liked my new dad. He built Lego with me. My old one never even had no Lego.'

'Stupid Lego,' muttered Sean.

'Well if you thought that was stupid, Sean, why don't you show Adrian the kind of Lego you like to build?'

He shrugged and carried on eating his dinner.

'Well the mum's got to learn the name of my cuddlies,' sighed Mary. 'I think it's going to take her a long time, Maggie.'

'I'm sure you can teach her.' I smiled.

That night before they went to bed, I got the children to fill a box each with some of their things.

'Not your really precious things, just stuff that Gillian and Adrian can take back to their house tomorrow when they come,' I explained. 'Then it will be really nice when you go to your new house and some of your things will already be there.'

All three looked unsure, but they dutifully picked a few toys and books to go in their boxes.

I could see the children were exhausted after the day's events, and all three were much quieter than usual as I put them to bed. When I went to check on Mary, she had silent tears running down her face.

'Oh, lovey,' I sighed, sitting down on her bed. 'What is it?'

'I don't know, but my tummy's hurting,' she sobbed, cuddling close to me.

'It's probably just all the excitement of the day,' I soothed, stroking her hair. 'And I bet you felt a bit nervous meeting your forever family didn't you?'

Mary nodded.

'Well, we'll see them again tomorrow and this time you'll already know them a little bit so it will be easier for everyone,' I reassured her.

'Will you be there, Maggie?' she asked, a worried look on her face.

'Of course I will.' I smiled. 'Now you try and get some sleep.'

I knew it was overwhelming for all three children. For months we'd been talking about their forever family and building this moment up and now they'd finally met them. The handover was always an unsettling time for children as it felt like they were in limbo. They knew they were letting go of me and leaving but they didn't really know the people that they were going to live with yet. After everything that these three had been through in their short little lives, I knew the process was going to be hard for everyone. I knew the most important thing was to reassure them and try to support them as much as possible.

By the time everyone was asleep, I was mentally and physically exhausted. I was tempted to get into bed myself, but when I looked at my mobile, I had a missed call from Lisa, and knew I should ring her back.

'So how did it go after Marie and I had left?' she asked excitedly when she picked up the phone.

'It was OK,' I sighed, struggling to keep the tiredness out of my voice. 'We had a few ups and downs, but I think everybody's getting used to each other. It's just going to take a bit of time, I suppose.'

'Well tomorrow's a new day, Maggie, so let's see what that brings,' she told me brightly. 'I'm sure the children will be delighted to see Gillian and Adrian again.'

I wished I could have shared her optimism.

Today had been a challenge for everyone and adrenaline and nerves had been running high. If I was being brutally honest, as far as first meetings go, it had felt like really hard work to me. I reminded myself that I hadn't done an adoption with older children for quite a while, which might have made it seem more strained. Babies and toddlers are so much easier to play with and get a response from.

As hard as it was to admit, I hadn't naturally warmed to Adrian and Gillian either. I couldn't put my finger on exactly what it was, but I couldn't help but frown as I remembered how eagerly the two of them had rushed to leave my house that evening. But I also had to remember they were coming from a life with no children to being around three demanding and damaged siblings, and that was a huge change. Maybe everyone just needed time to adapt. I hoped that tomorrow would go more smoothly.

But as I tossed and turned in bed that night, I couldn't shake the feeling of doubt nagging away at me.

THIRTEEN

Niggles and Doubts

The next morning I was making breakfast when my mobile rang. I was surprised to see Carol's name flashing up on the screen.

'I hope you don't mind me calling, Maggie, but I was desperate to know how it went yesterday,' she said apologetically, when I picked up. 'You and the kids were on my mind all day.'

'It went OK I think,' I sighed, keeping my voice low. 'It's really difficult to tell. No one ran away or had a meltdown so I suppose in that way it was good.'

'What about Sean?' she asked anxiously. 'How did he cope with it all?'

'He largely ignored them and was generally very quiet,' I told her. 'He was just weighing them up and trying to get his head around it all, I think. As we expected, Dougie and Mary were a lot more involved with them.'

'And what were the couple like with the kids?' asked Carol. 'I bet they were completely taken with them.'

'To be honest, they were a little bit stiff and awkward,' I told her. 'They didn't really seem to know how to act around them, and I got the sense that they couldn't get out of here fast enough.'

I hesitated.

'I'm probably being really unfair,' I sighed. 'I'm sure things will be easier today and they'll be a little bit more relaxed when they come round.'

'I'm sure you're right,' Carol agreed.

While the children got dressed, I had a quick tidy up and moved the boxes the kids had packed the night before into the hallway. I'd just finished carrying them downstairs when Adrian and Gillian arrived.

'Morning.' I smiled. 'Come on in.'

I saw them clocking the boxes piled up by the front door.

'Oh, have you packed their stuff already?' asked Gillian, looking surprised.

'No, these are just a few bits and pieces,' I explained. 'I'll probably send a few boxes back with you every time you see the children.'

'Oh, how many boxes do you think there's going to be?' She frowned.

'I don't really know. Probably most days you'll have this amount to take and there's their clothes as well.'

'Oh OK,' she sighed disapprovingly. 'It sounds like they've got quite the collection of things.'

Looking at her expression, I couldn't help but feel as if I was being criticised for them having too much stuff.

'Shall I make you a tea or a coffee?' I asked, quickly changing the subject. 'The children are just getting dressed and they'll be down in a moment.'

'That would be lovely,' said Adrian.

We were just settling down with a coffee when Dougie came hurtling into the room.

'Hello, new daddy,' he yelled and started swinging off his arms and clinging onto his legs.

Adrian looked startled, and I sensed that it was all a bit too much having Dougie clambering all over him. I didn't want him to feel uncomfortable, so I gently peeled Dougie off.

'Dougie, sweetie, why don't you let Adrian have his coffee, then I'm sure he'll play with you.'

'How about we all go out to the park?' I suggested, once Mary and Sean had come downstairs.

'Yay!' screeched Dougie loudly. 'Let's go!'

I noticed Gillian flinch and I couldn't help but think that she'd have to get used to the noise with three children around.

On the walk there, I quietly encouraged the children to walk with Adrian and Gillian rather than me.

'But I want to walk with you,' said Mary.

'Me too,' sighed Dougie.

Sean marched off on his own in front while Dougie and Mary grabbed my hands and Adrian and Gillian walked behind us. When we got there, I sat down on a bench.

'Maggie, will you push me on the swing?' asked Dougie, tugging at my skirt.

'No, lovey, I'm tired,' I told him gently. 'I'm just going to sit here for a bit. Why don't you go and play?'

I was desperate for Adrian and Gillian to take over. I wanted them to push the children on the swings, help Dougie on the big slide and pull the roundabout round for them. I wanted them to do all of the things that parents do for their children.

After a few minutes, though, I could see that they were trying their hardest. Sean was sitting sulkily on the roundabout and Adrian walked over and sat next to him. He started chatting to him and pointing at the trees. My heart leapt as the two of them got up and started walking around the outskirts of the park looking at some of the plants and flowers. It was the first time I'd seen Sean interact with either of them, and I let out a sigh of relief. Maybe everything was going to be OK after all.

Eventually Sean ran off to play on the climbing frame and Adrian walked over to me.

'He's very knowledgeable, isn't he?' He smiled. 'He's just been telling me all about butterflies.'

'Oh yes, he's very into animals and nature.' I nodded proudly. 'He's a clever lad.'

I was pleased that they'd found a common ground and had something to talk about.

Adrian wandered back off in the direction of the climbing frame, and I peered around to see what the others were up to.

Gillian was pushing Mary on the swing, and I could hear Mary giggling as she swung higher and higher.

'I want a go too,' yelled Dougie, hanging off Gillian's arm. I could see Gillian was uncomfortable with him climbing all over her and she didn't seem to know quite how to handle it.

She hesitated a moment, then picked Dougie up and put him in a toddler swing.

Oh dear, he's not going to like that, I thought to myself.

Sure enough, Dougie immediately started kicking and struggling, desperately trying to escape the little swing.

'No, no, not this one!' he shouted.

'Those ones,' he said, pointing to the swings that Mary was on.

'No, Dougie, they're far too big for you,' Gillian told him firmly.

'But I always go on them ones,' he yelled, kicking at her furiously.

I could see he was about to have a meltdown so I hurried over to them before Dougie lost it completely.

'He'll be OK on the big swings,' I murmured to Gillian. 'He's quite careful and he knows to hold onto the ropes.'

'Oh, OK,' she said. 'Sorry.'

'You don't have to apologise,' I reassured her, patting her arm and smiling. 'You didn't know.'

She hurried over to the toddler swings and scooped Dougie out. Thankfully, he stopped crying immediately, and was soon swinging happily as Gillian began pushing both him and Mary.

They were both chattering away to her but I couldn't help but notice that she wasn't saying much to them in return. She definitely wasn't what I'd call natural with them, but I reasoned that maybe she just needed some time to relax.

On the way back from the park, Dougie begged Adrian to carry him.

'I'm tired,' he sighed, dragging his feet and trailing behind the others.

'How about I give you a piggy back?' suggested Adrian, kneeling beside him.

'No darling, put him down – he needs to learn to walk,' Gillian told him firmly.

Much to Dougie's disappointment, Adrian did as his wife asked, though he did hold Dougie's hand for the rest of the walk home.

We went home and after a quiet lunch, Adrian and Gillian left. The following day was Sunday so everyone was having a day apart to recover.

The children seemed as relieved as I was, and I made sure that we had a low-key day in the house after all of the emotion of the last couple of days. All three seemed more subdued than usual, but I put it down to them being tired.

Part of the settling-in period was about the adoptive couple getting to know the children's routine. So on Monday morning they came at 7.30 a.m. to help get the children dressed and ready and walk them to school.

I went downstairs and deliberately left them to it as I didn't want to interfere. Louisa had stayed at Charlie's all weekend and it was the first time that she had met Adrian and Gillian.

'They seem very polite and smartly dressed, but they're so serious,' she whispered to me once they'd gone upstairs.

'They're very nice people and they're trying really hard,' I told her firmly.

As we both made breakfast, I could hear shouting and banging coming from upstairs.

'No, I am not getting dressed,' I heard Sean shouting.

After another five minutes of continuous banging and yelling, I knew I had to go and intervene.

I looked through the door to a scene of utter chaos. Dougie was half dressed in his pyjama bottoms and school shirt, while Sean was still in his pyjamas. Clothes were flung all over the floor and both boys were laughing and jumping on their beds.

'Sean, get dressed now,' I heard Gillian shout.

'No,' he yelled. 'I'm not getting dressed. Maggie lets me get dressed after breakfast.'

I knew he was trying it on.

I stepped into the room and cleared my throat. Both boys glanced at me sheepishly, but carried on bouncing.

'Get down off the beds now,' I told them firmly. 'You know you don't bounce on the bed or climb on the furniture.

'Come on, Sean, you know it's time for you to get dressed. You're not going down to breakfast until your clothes are on.'

Both boys immediately got down.

'Then when we come back upstairs after breakfast we do our . . .

'Teeth!' shouted Dougie enthusiastically.

Once the boys had got dressed, I sent them downstairs.

'They wouldn't listen to us,' sighed Adrian, looking stressed.

'They were being very difficult,' snapped Gillian, an exasperated look on her face.

'It's still early days,' I reassured them. 'They're pushing the boundaries and trying it on with you. You should have seen how they behaved when they first came to live with me. When you're adopting children like them, you have to be prepared for challenging behaviour.'

'Oh I'm sure they'll settle down once they're with us full time,' Gillian replied, dismissing everything I'd just said. I couldn't help but feel a flicker of annoyance.

After another day's break, Gillian and Adrian were going to pick the children up from school and take them back to their house for tea.

'Won't it be exciting to see your new house?' I smiled at the children over breakfast that morning.

Mary and Dougie nodded and gave me a weak smile, while Sean played listlessly with his cereal. I could see all three of them were absolutely shattered. The settling-in process was clearly taking its toll.

That afternoon when pick-up time rolled around, it felt strange not having to rush out and collect the children. The house felt eerily quiet and I didn't quite know what to do with myself. I took the opportunity to catch up on some paperwork in an attempt to keep busy and take my mind off the kids. I couldn't stop thinking about them and worrying about how it was going at Gillian and Adrian's house.

I couldn't wait to see how it had gone when they came in that night. They all walked in very quietly and solemnly.

'Did you have a lovely time?' I asked them, smiling enthusiastically. 'Was it brilliant to see your new house?'

'Sean was really naughty,' sighed Mary. 'And Adrian and Gillian got dead cross.'

'Oh dear, that's a shame. But I'm sure your new mummy and daddy have dealt with it.'

It was important that they started to recognise that Gillian and Adrian were in charge when they were with them and it wasn't right for me to interfere. They seemed exhausted so I got them all to bed.

'Apart from Sean being naughty, was it great seeing your new house?' I asked Mary when I went to tuck her in. 'Did you love your new bedroom?'

'It was OK.' She shrugged. 'Maggie, there was a big wooden box in there and all my cuddlies were inside it. I told Gillian I wanted them on my bed like I have here but she said it's too messy. They can't breathe in a box, can they, Maggie?'

'Of course they can, lovey,' I reassured her. 'They're magic and they can live anywhere.'

From what I'd seen so far, Gillian seemed to be obsessed by cleanliness and tidiness. But you couldn't be that way when you had three children in the house, especially children like these three. I could see that Gillian and Adrian were finding it difficult to cope with the children testing the boundaries, and I dreaded to think what might happen when they had them at home full time and, as often happened, some of the siblings' old behaviours came back. How would they cope then?

When I went to bed that night, my head was spinning. The niggling doubts were getting stronger and I was starting to have so many worries about the way things were going.

Halfway through the night I was woken up by a noise. It sounded like whimpering. I walked out onto the landing and realised it was coming from the boys' room. I went in to find Sean curled up in a ball on his bed, whimpering and shivering.

'What is it, sweetie?' I whispered gently.

It was then that I realised he was soaking wet and was shivering with cold.

'Oh, lovey, you've wet the bed,' I told him. 'Let's get you up and sort you out.'

'I'm sorry,' he whimpered. 'I didn't mean to. Please don't be cross.'

'Of course I'm not cross,' I soothed.

I quickly changed his sheets and helped him into a pair of clean pyjamas. Thankfully now he was dry he'd warmed up a bit.

'You try and get some more sleep,' I murmured, pulling his duvet over him and tucking him in.

As I lay in bed my mind was racing. Despite all his toilet-training issues in the past, he's never once wet the bed and I knew it was caused by his anxiety about the adoption.

A couple of nights later, the children went back to Adrian and Gillian's after school. Again, all three were very quiet when they came back.

'They got a bit upset because they wanted to do sticking and gluing but I thought it was a bit babyish for them so I said no,' Gillian told me brusquely, as she dropped them off.

'Actually, all three of them really enjoy quite simple things like sticking and gluing and potato printing,' I explained. 'They missed out on so much play when they were younger that sometimes it's nice for them to do messy play or even Play-Doh.'

'Well I think they preferred the painting in the end anyway,' Gillian replied sniffily, sticking to her guns.

That night after Gillian and Adrian had gone, I gave Dougie a bath.

'Did you see the new book that I sneaked into the pile of books that I sent to your new house?'

I'd bought him a new one all about dinosaurs because I knew he loved them.

'No, I'm not allowed to touch the books,' he sighed, fiddling with a toy boat.

'What do you mean?' I asked, surprised.

'My new mummy puts them on a high shelf downstairs and we're not allowed to touch them in case they get ripped. We're allowed to choose one at bedtime and my new mummy or daddy reads it with us.'

I was shocked, as Dougie was actually quite careful these days, and I always let the kids choose books to look at.

The following morning when the children had gone to school, Becky called me.

'I just thought I'd check in with you and see how the settling in is going,' she said. 'How are the children coping?'

'OK,' I told her cautiously. 'I'm hoping things will start to improve.'

'It's early days,' she reminded me.

'Yes, I know it takes time to adjust. It's just . . .'

My voice trailed off.

'It's just what, Maggie?' Becky asked.

I took a deep breath and at last, I said the words I'd been thinking for the past few days. The words I hadn't dared say up until now.

'I just don't think it's working,' I blurted out. 'Becky, I'm really not sure that this couple is the right match for the children.'

'Gosh,' Becky exclaimed, clearly shocked. 'What makes you say that?'

'Lots of things,' I sighed. 'Lots of niggly things that have made me question it.'

'Have you raised your concerns with Lisa and Marie?' she asked.

'I've made a few comments, but I've not said it explicitly,' I told her. 'There's no point. I know what they'll say. They'll tell me that it's just a time thing and that it will take time for everyone to adjust.'

'Well they're probably right, Maggie,' Becky told me gently.

'Maybe they are, and of course I really do hope that is the case, but I've done enough adoptions in twenty-odd years to know when one just doesn't feel right. It kills me to say it because I so want things to work out for everyone. These children deserve to have a happy ending. I'm just having major doubts that it's with Adrian and Gillian.'

'But what is it exactly, Maggie?' asked Becky, clearly concerned. 'Have they done something wrong?'

'Not as such,' I sighed. 'It's just a funny niggling feeling that I have that I can't ignore any longer. They seem very focused on cleanliness and tidiness, which are two things that are probably going to go out of the window when three children go and live with them. And I'm worried they're just not prepared for the behavioural problems they're going to have with the kids.

'We're over a week in and everything still feels very forced and stilted,' I continued. 'The children are exhausted and all the initial excitement they had about finding their forever family has gone. Now they just seem to be relieved to come back to my house.

'Gillian and Adrian seem to disregard anything I say and think they know best. They refuse to engage in any conversation about the children's behavioural issues. They're going to get them home and I'll guarantee the children will put them through hell. I honestly don't think they're prepared for that and I don't think they're going to know how to cope with it.'

I could tell Becky was shocked by my outburst.

'Perhaps it's just that Gillian and Adrian are not your kind of people?' she suggested. 'It doesn't mean that they're not going to be good adoptive parents to the kids. The fact is, Maggie, they've been approved by a panel. They are going to be their parents and they're going to have their way of doing things and you're going to have your way of doing things. At the end of the day, if the adoption worker and the kids' social worker are happy with the way things are going, there's not a lot you can do about it.'

'I know,' I sighed.

The harsh reality was that as a foster carer, I could give my opinion but ultimately it was the social worker who made the final decision.

'The hard thing is, we're not going to truly know if this is going to work until the children are with them full time,' sighed Becky. 'Don't hate me, Maggie, but I think everyone is right. You just need to give it time. You've got to appreciate that it must feel strange for them coming into somebody else's house. The children obviously have a natural affection for you. Affection is something that grows, and you know as well as I do that it doesn't come instantly, especially with children like these who have attachment issues.

'Maybe when they get the children home and they can spend time together in their own surroundings things will be different.'

'I know what you're saying,' I told Becky reluctantly. 'I only hope that you're right.'

But as I hung up the phone, my conversation with Becky had done very little to prevent my growing sense of unease. As more time passed, every bone in my body was telling me that this adoption wasn't going to work.

It was very rare for me to feel like this and I desperately wanted to be proved wrong.

A couple of weeks into the settling-in process, everyone gathered at my house while the children were at school for a planning meeting to discuss the next steps. Gillian and Adrian were there, as well as Lisa, Becky and Marie, the adoption officer, and Julie the IRO.

'I had a chat with Adrian and Gillian before we came in today and it sounds like everything's going brilliantly.' Julie smiled. 'How are you finding things, Maggie?'

Everyone looked at me expectantly.

'Um, if I'm being honest, I think it's been very hard,' I sighed. 'The children are taking more time than I would have expected to adjust and everyone still seems quite tense with each other.'

'Well, I haven't found that, have you, Adrian?' Gillian jumped in at once.

'No,' he agreed. 'We think it's going really well. As far as we're concerned the children are doing brilliantly. If there's any tension at all it's when we bring them back to Maggie's and they're upset because they want to come back with us.'

I couldn't believe my ears.

'I know Sean is finding it very difficult to adjust,' I told Julie.

'Yes, Sean has been a bit awkward,' agreed Gillian. 'However, I think it's because he's unsettled. I think the sooner the children are with us permanently, the better.'

'I think you're right,' nodded Lisa. 'The settling-in period can be a funny time for children.'

'Well I think we're all agreed it's full steam ahead with this adoption then,' said Julie, closing her file. 'I'm pleased that you're happy, Adrian and Gillian, with the way things are going and I'm sure as time goes on, Sean will start to feel more settled.'

Everyone nodded and smiled, and it was clear the meeting was over. As everyone filed out, chatting politely, I hung back, not wanting to make conversation.

After the meeting, I felt uneasy. I had tried to voice my concerns but had been shut down immediately. I couldn't help but feel like the baddy and almost as if it was my fault. I started questioning myself.

Maybe I was the problem, not Gillian and Adrian? Perhaps it was going well and I was too attached to the children so I was struggling to let them go?

But deep down I knew that wasn't the case. My doubts were very real and growing by the day. All I knew was that I needed to say something and I needed to say it soon. But would anyone be prepared to listen? Or was it all too late?

FOURTEEN

A Difficult Goodbye

My hands were shaking as I gripped the phone and dialled Lisa's number. I took a deep breath as she answered.

'Oh, hi, Maggie,' she said casually. 'How are you?'

'Lisa, I'm ringing because there's something I want to discuss with you,' I told her, unable to disguise the urgent tone in my voice. 'It's something really important.'

'Yes, of course,' she replied, suddenly sounding concerned. 'Is everything OK? Is something wrong with one of the children?'

I felt my stomach churning with nerves as I said what had been preying on my mind these past few weeks.

'I've agonised about whether to say anything to you,' I babbled. 'But the thing is . . .'

I hesitated. Was this really the right thing to do?

'The thing is,' I continued. 'I'm having major doubts about this adoption. Lisa, I'm really worried. I don't think it's going to work.'

'But why, Maggie?' she gasped, sounding shocked. 'I thought things were going really well?'

'I suppose it's just a feeling I have,' I sighed. 'Gillian and Adrian are very different people to me, which is absolutely fine. But I've tried to be honest with them about the children. About how bad their behaviour was when they first came to me, how they might regress for a while when they move in with them and how they might struggle to attach after everything they've been through. I'm worried they'll both struggle to cope but they don't seem to believe anything that I'm telling them.'

'Maggie, I can assure you that we've told them all of that,' said Lisa, sounding frustrated. 'Gillian and Adrian are going into this with their eyes wide open. We've been very honest and upfront about the children's background.'

'It's not just that,' I pressed on, determined to say my bit. 'They're very rigid and Gillian in particular seems obsessed with cleanliness and hygiene. I feel like the children are walking on eggshells around them.'

'These kids are not the perfect, ready-made family that I think Gillian wants,' I ploughed on, my voice tinged with desperation. 'The reality is they are three damaged children with attachment issues. They're going to bring mess, noise and chaos. They're going to turn their life as they know it upside down and I'm worried that they're not prepared for that.'

'Oh, Maggie,' sighed Lisa, in a voice that couldn't have been more patronising if she had tried. 'I think this is more about you and your difficulty letting these children go. I know you're incredibly fond of them. Perhaps no one is ever going to be good enough for them in your eyes?'

I felt tears of anger rising up in my throat and I took a deep breath to compose myself.

'Lisa, believe me when I say I honestly don't think it's that,' I told her firmly. 'Of course saying goodbye is always going to be hard but I've done this enough times over the years to know how to let children go. I want nothing more than for the children to get their happy ending.'

'What are you saying then, Maggie?' asked Lisa seriously.

'Something doesn't feel right,' I replied. 'Perhaps we have to accept that it's too soon for them to be adopted or that this couple isn't the right match for these kids? I hate to say it but every bone in my body is telling me that this isn't going to work.'

'I'm sorry, Maggie, but it's gone too far now,' Lisa told me matter-of-factly. 'The children are days away from leaving. They seem happy to Marie and me, and Adrian and Gillian are telling us that everything is going well. I'm afraid you're a lone voice in all of this.'

She paused.

'This adoption is going to happen, Maggie, and the sooner you get used to that, the better.'

I felt so frustrated and confused. The reality was I didn't wield enough power to stop this. As a foster carer, my views would always be taken into consideration but ultimately, I couldn't change Social Service's decision. I could kick up a fuss all I wanted but it was clear that it wasn't going to make any difference. I had to go along with it, even though I was the one who was with the children 24–7 and therefore knew them the best.

For once, I really hoped that I had got this dreadfully wrong.

'I'm sure things will be different when the children are with Adrian and Gillian full time,' Lisa continued brightly. 'You've said it yourself: with older kids this settling-in period can be very difficult when they're in between two houses.'

'I really hope so,' I sighed, trying to keep my voice steady.

'I know it's difficult, Maggie, but I understand, I really do,' Lisa soothed in the same tone of voice that she spoke to the children with. 'You've done such a good job with them and I know it's hard to say goodbye.

'I will be going out to see the children once they've moved and keeping an eye on things so don't you worry.'

I felt like I was being given a pat on the head and told to go away. My concerns had been well and truly dismissed. All I could do was put my doubts to one side and throw myself into making this work.

But it's hard when you're not behind something 100 per cent. Normally I loved overseeing adoptions. It was always intense and at times it was stressful. Inevitably there were always going to be difficulties, but it was such a privilege to see the love and affection grow between the adopters and the children. The problem was that I wasn't picking up on any of that here.

These days the children were strangely quiet and reserved, and even Sean had stopped his outbursts, which to be honest was even more worrying to me, as it was so out of character. We were well over two weeks into the settling-in period now and they were having their first overnight stay at their new house.

Gillian and Adrian dropped them back the following night after school.

'How did it go?' I asked.

All three children looked exhausted and there were dark hollows under their eyes, which told me they hadn't slept well. Gillian and Adrian looked equally drained.

Dougie came running in and flung himself into my lap.

'Sean did swearing and my new mummy got cross and had to tell him off,' he told me.

'Oh dear, that's a shame. Still, I'm sure your new mummy and daddy have dealt with it,' I told him, trying to reinforce Gillian and Adrian's authority.

'Did you have a lovely time staying at the house though?'

Dougie nodded uncertainly but didn't say anything.

I didn't ask Sean about what had happened. I knew it was best if I kept out of it completely. It was important that I let Gillian and Adrian deal with it.

When the children had gone upstairs, I spoke to Gillian.

'If it makes you feel any better, Sean swore an awful lot when he first came here,' I told her. 'His language was atrocious. I found the best way to deal with it was not to make a fuss. I knew it was learnt behaviour and that eventually it would stop. Now he only swears when he's anxious or when he's fearful rather than actually doing it to be naughty or aggressive.'

'Well, we made it very clear to him that we're not going to tolerate that kind of foul language in our house,' said Gillian brusquely.

'It's so difficult,' I said sympathetically. 'Do you want to have a chat about it properly later? I could call you when the kids are in bed?'

'No, no it's fine. We're just not willing to accept swearing full stop.'

When Gillian and Adrian had gone I went upstairs to check on the children.

'So was it really exciting sleeping at your new house for the very first time?' I asked Mary. 'Do you think you're going to be happy there?'

'I like my new bedroom,' she said quietly.

'And what about your new mummy and daddy?' I said. 'Do you think you'll be happy with them?'

She hesitated.

'Yes, I think I like them,' she said unconvincingly.

She paused and gave me a weak smile.

'Maggie, will we still see you?' she asked, her eyes wide in the dark.

'Yes of course you will, flower,' I reassured her. 'Louisa and I have already arranged with Lisa that in a few weeks we'll come and visit you at your new house. Then you can show me your lovely new bedroom.'

I was doing my best to reassure the children that everything was going to be OK, but it was hard when I had my own doubts about what was happening.

That night when Louisa got in from work we were chatting in the kitchen.

'I can't believe the kids are leaving in a couple of days,' she sighed. 'It feels so strange.'

'The house is going to be very quiet,' I agreed.

I hadn't shared any of my concerns about the adoption with her as I didn't want to worry her. I didn't think it was fair to burden her with my fears.

'What shall we do to say goodbye to them?' she asked. 'Why don't we have a little tea party like we sometimes do when children leave?'

I shook my head.

'They've been so unsettled by the changes and they're so overwhelmed by everything at the moment that I think it's probably best to keep it really low-key,' I explained.

We decided that we'd all go out to Pizza Hut for tea as a special goodbye treat. I invited Carol and my friend Vicky and her foster children.

The next few days were all about goodbyes. The children had their last day at school and they all came home with a card from each of their classes that everyone had signed. Each of Dougie's classmates had done a handprint for him to remember them by.

Most of their stuff had gone over to Adrian and Gillian's by now and they had spent the odd night at their new house but they were still living with me. Finally it was time for them to officially move in with their new parents. So, after spending the night with Adrian and Gillian, they dropped them back for their last evening with us. It was the last night the children would be sleeping at my house.

Before we went out, Mary insisted on getting changed. It made me smile to see what a girly girl she had become during her time with me.

'Maggie, will you put my hair in a plait?' she asked me when I stuck my head around her bedroom door to see where she'd got to.

Louisa had taught her how to do it herself but she'd never asked me before.

'I don't think I'm very good at plaits, but I'll give it a try,' I told her.

She gave me a weak smile and handed me a hairbrush and a bobble. She sat on her bed with her back to me and I gently brushed her long, light brown hair. It was so soft and silky and smelt of strawberry shampoo – so different to when she had first arrived.

I carefully divided her hair into three sections.

'You know our mum in prison?' she asked me as I started to plait it. 'Does she know that we've got a new mummy and daddy?'

'Yes, lovey,' I told her. 'Social Services will have told them about Gillian and Adrian.'

'So will they come and visit us when they get out?' she asked.

'No, sweetie,' I reassured her. 'Once you're adopted, it means that you're part of that new family.'

'So when they get out they can't just come and get us and take us back to the flat can they?' she asked anxiously.

'Definitely not,' I promised. 'They wouldn't know where to come and get you from because no one is allowed to tell them your new address.'

Understandably she was trying to get everything straight in her little head.

'All finished.' I smiled, tying a bobble at the bottom of the plait to secure it. 'Shall we go and get some pizza now?'

She smiled and nodded, squeezing my hand as we walked downstairs.

I swallowed the lump in my throat as I realised that this was the last night she'd be staying with me.

As we drove to Pizza Hut for our final meal, I tried to put my feelings to one side and focus on making sure the children were happy and settled. For once Sean was being very quiet, and Dougie was being extremely clingy. He wanted to constantly sit on my knee during dinner and he was clambering on me and giving me cuddles. I knew he was seeking reassurance.

'Oh I'm going to miss your cuddles so much.' I smiled, cuddling him tight. 'But tomorrow's going to be a very exciting day, isn't it? You're going to go and live in your new house with your new mummy and daddy.'

After we were all stuffed to the brim with pizza and ice cream, I knew it was time to go back and get the children's last few things together ready for the morning when Gillian and Adrian came to collect them.

On the way out as we walked to the car, Mary grabbed my hand and skipped along next to me.

'Can we come here again, Maggie?' she asked. 'I really liked it.'

'I'm sure if you ask your new mummy and daddy, they'll take you,' I replied.

I saw her little face drop.

'Oh, I forgot we were going away tomorrow,' she sighed, looking away.

My heart broke at the disappointment in her voice.

When we got home I took them upstairs to get ready for bed. Their rooms looked very bare now as most of their things were packed up or had already gone over to Gillian and Adrian's.

'My bedroom looks really funny,' sighed Mary sadly when I went to tuck her in. 'There's only Sparkle left.'

She'd kept her favourite soft toy unicorn with her until last so she was going to take him in the morning. She cuddled him close and I noticed her eyes had filled up with tears.

'Sparkle's gonna miss your house, Maggie,' she sighed.

'Oh Sparkle will be just fine, I'm sure of it,' I told her gently. 'He's going to have lots of fun at his new house.'

'But Sparkle loves you so much, Maggie, and he wants to stay with you,' Mary whispered, a tear rolling down her cheek.

'Oh, Sparkle,' I sighed, pretending to talk to the unicorn. 'I'm going to miss you too, but you're going to have a lovely time in your new house with your new family. And Louisa and I will come and see you and check that you're OK,' I promised, patting his head.

'Do you think he feels better?' I asked Mary.

She nodded and wiped away her tears.

'Now you get some sleep, young lady, because it's a big day tomorrow.' I smiled, giving her a hug.

When I went to say goodnight to the boys, Dougie looked exhausted and was almost asleep. Sean on the other hand seemed agitated and was pacing up and down.

'I want to play Lego,' he huffed. 'Where's my Lego?'

'It's packed away in the box all ready for you to take tomorrow,' I reminded him.

'But I want to play it now,' he yelled, kicking the bed.

'It's bedtime now, Sean,' I told him firmly.

'I don't want to go to f****ng bed,' he snapped, throwing himself on the floor. 'Why did you pack it away, you b**ch?'

As hard as it was to see him like this, I knew that he was making himself dislike me to make it easier for himself to let go and move on. A lot of children did this when they were being adopted so in a way I took it as a good sign.

'Come on, Sean. Get into bed please.'

Thankfully he did as I'd asked and reluctantly crawled under the covers. I tucked him in and sat down on the bed beside him.

'I know this is a big change for you, lovey, and it's really hard, but it will all be OK,' I soothed.

He looked up at me, his eyes wide with fear.

Suddenly all his bravado had disappeared and he looked like a scared and vulnerable little boy.

'What if we don't like it at their house?' he asked in a small voice. 'Can we come back?'

'It will be absolutely fine,' I reassured him. 'Your new mummy and daddy can't wait for you all to be a family.'

It was so hard convincing them that everything was going to be fine when I was struggling to convince myself. No matter what I thought, I had to reassure them that everything was going to be OK.

'You were ages up there,' said Louisa, when I finally came downstairs. 'Are they all right?'

'I think it's all hitting home that they're leaving. Sean and Mary were having a wobble but I know they will all be fine in the end,' I sighed.

Again, because the children had been so up and down, I hadn't wanted to give them presents and cards and make a big deal about them leaving. I'd got them a little gift each that I was going to put in with their things so they'd find it when they unpacked at their new house.

'Shall I help you wrap them?' asked Louisa.

'That would be great.' I smiled, grateful as always to have Louisa around.

I'd got the boys a Lego set each and Mary a pottery teapot and cup set that she could paint. While Louisa wrapped them, I wrote them a little note each.

I thought you might like to do this with your new mummy and daddy. Miss you lots. Love always, Maggie and Louisa xx, I wrote on each of the labels.

As Louisa read the notes, her eyes filled up.

'Oh I'm going to miss them too,' she sighed. 'They were a complete nightmare when they arrived but I've grown to love the little monkeys.'

'I know you have, lovey,' I said, giving her hand a squeeze.

I never underestimated how hard it was for Louisa to say goodbye to the children that I fostered, as they were a big part of her life too.

That night as I lay in bed, my stomach churned with a mix of nerves and anticipation. I never liked saying goodbye but I normally got an enormous sense of pride and satisfaction when children moved on to a new life with a new family. This time I just had a lingering feeling of dread.

All night I tossed and turned, unable to sleep with all the thoughts whirring around my brain. I was exhausted by the morning and I felt like a zombie as I made the children breakfast and rushed around the house packing up the last of their things.

'There's a little surprise for each of you in your boxes,' I told them. 'So make sure you have a look later.'

Gillian and Adrian arrived early to pick the children up, and I could see they were excited.

'How are you feeling?' I asked them brightly.

'We can't wait to get them home and start our new life together,' smiled Gillian.

'Well, they're all ready for you,' I told them.

Dougie, bless him, seemed really excited while Mary and Sean were very quiet.

'Maggie took us to a place called Pizza Hut for our tea last night,' Mary told them shyly. 'Can we go there one time?'

'Yeah, can we go to Pizza Hut?' yelled Dougie, jumping up and down.

Yes, of course we'll take you out for dinner,' said Gillian. 'But we don't really do Pizza Hut.'

I busied myself helping to carry the children's last few boxes to the car with Adrian while Louisa said her goodbyes to them. Adrian must have sensed my anxiety.

'I'm sure they're going to be fine, Maggie,' he said to me. 'We'll give you a ring and let you know how they are.'

'Thank you,' I replied, meaning it. 'I'd really appreciate that.'

Back inside, there was no delaying the inevitable. It was time for me to say my goodbyes. I squeezed each of the children tight, savouring the feeling of their little bodies in my arms for the very last time.

'I'll miss you lots but I'll see you all very soon,' I promised, kissing the tops of their heads.

'Bye Maggie and Louisa,' grinned Dougie.

Mary and Sean didn't say a word and stared at the floor.

I had to try my hardest to fight back the tears.

'Come on then,' Gillian told them briskly, eager to get off. 'Let's get you three home.'

As Louisa and I stood on the doorstep and waved them off, I felt churned up inside. It was always upsetting to say goodbye and feel the almost-physical pain of loss but this was more than that. There was no sense of satisfaction that I'd done a good job. I was just overwhelmed by doubt and worry.

Louisa must have seen my anxious face.

'They're going to be OK, Maggie,' she reassured me, squeezing my hand.

'I hope so,' I sighed, swallowing the lump in my throat.

Louisa went inside to get ready for work while I waited to watch Adrian and Gillian's car pull away. As they drove off down the street, I saw Sean's worried little face looking back at me from the back seat. He looked terrified.

The car disappeared off down the street and they were gone.

Oh God, please let it be OK, I told myself.

As soon as Louisa had left, I closed the front door and finally allowed myself to let my guard down. The fake smile that I'd plastered on my face all morning was gone and my heart was heavy.

I leant back against the front door and slid down it. Sitting on the hard floorboards of the hallway, I put my head in my hands and sobbed. Every part of me was telling me that this adoption wasn't going to work and I hoped to God that I had got it wrong.

FIFTEEN

Keeping Clear

As Louisa flicked through the catalogue, I felt my mind wandering.

'What do you think, Maggie?' she asked. 'Shall I choose one with a full skirt or go a bit more modern and slinky?'

'Sorry, lovey?' I asked, realising I hadn't got a clue what she was talking about. 'What did you say?'

'Oh, Maggie, are you all right?' she sighed, sounding concerned. 'You were miles away. I was talking about wedding dresses. Do you think I should have a big pooty one or go more fitted?'

'I don't know, flower,' I replied vaguely. 'It's up to you.'

In all honesty, wedding dresses were the last thing on my mind. The children had been gone three days now and I had been a ball of worry and anxiety ever since. They'd been on my mind constantly and I was worried about how they were and how it was going. I'd had one text from Lisa telling me that she'd popped in and everything was fine but I'd heard nothing from Gillian or Adrian.

'Now the children have left I think I'm going to have a couple of weeks off to clear my head,' I told Louisa.

'That's brilliant,' she exclaimed. 'You can come to the wedding fair with me and Charlie, and we can maybe go wedding dress shopping?'

'Of course.' I smiled. 'I'd absolutely love that.'

Maybe a bit of wedding planning was exactly what I needed to take my mind off things. Louisa and Charlie had been engaged for over a year. They were still saving up for a flat but they'd got fed up of waiting and decided to take the plunge and book their big day. It was still over a year away but Louisa was desperate to crack on with the plans and I could see she was so excited. It was such a special time for her and I didn't want to put a dampener on it.

Later that morning, Becky rang me.

'I'm just checking in to see how you're doing,' she said brightly.

'Not great, to be honest,' I sighed. 'I can't shake the feeling that I've let the children down.'

'Maggie, don't torment yourself,' she told me firmly. 'You've done your bit, now it's Gillian and Adrian's turn. The children will be fine. Social Services seem happy so we've just got to assume that it's going well.'

'You're probably right,' I replied. 'I think I'm exhausted. It was quite an intense time looking after the three of them so I think I'm going to take a few weeks off. It will give me chance to clear my head, sort the house out and help Louisa with some wedding planning.

'I might even book a weekend away with Graham,' I added. 'I haven't seen the poor man much in the past few months.'

'I think that's a really good idea, Maggie,' agreed Becky. 'When you're feeling ready I can put you back on the available list. Knowing you, I bet you'll be ringing me up in a couple of days desperate for a new placement,' she laughed.

But in my heart I knew that wouldn't be the case. I didn't want to admit it to Louisa or Becky or anyone else, but I was determined to have a break and not take on any new placements and I knew exactly why. My gut was still telling me that the children's adoption wasn't going to work and I was deliberately keeping myself free just in case Sean, Dougie and Mary needed to come back. If it all went wrong, I felt like I owed it to them to take them back. Three children weren't easy to place and I hated the idea of them having to be split up and sent to different carers.

A couple of days later I got a text from Gillian. My heart thumped as I clicked on it.

Children fine. Sean a bit tricky but generally all OK x

It didn't do much to ease my worries.

'Generally OK?' I said to Carol when she popped in for a coffee that morning. 'What on earth does that mean? And it concerns me that Sean's being tricky. What do you think she means by that?'

'I don't know about you but I expected Sean to be tricky,' laughed Carol. 'I think I'd be more worried if he wasn't.'

'You're right,' I sighed. 'I'm probably overthinking it.'

That afternoon I tapped out a reply to her.

Thanks for letting me know. I'm here if you need to talk but glad it's going OK. Maggie xx

As the days passed, I kept myself busy to try and take my mind off things. One morning I rearranged the bedrooms and put all of the things back that I'd removed when the boys had first come to live with me, like the pendant light, the curtains and curtain pole and the pictures on the wall. I bought new bedding and a rug to change things up a bit.

I was putting a new duvet on one of the beds when I pulled something out from down the side of the mattress. It was a little Lego fireman.

'Oh, Dougie,' I sighed.

It was one of his favourites and I remembered that he'd been looking for that before he left. I felt a pang in my heart as I pictured his excited little face when he'd managed to build the fire engine with Sean for the first time. He'd been so proud. I put it in an envelope to keep it safe for him.

Everywhere I looked there were little reminders of the children. I met Graham for a drink at a country pub one night and when I reached in my handbag for a tissue, I fished out a little flowery clip and a bobble of Mary's instead.

I swallowed the lump in my throat and quickly shoved them back into my bag, but Graham must have noticed my reaction.

'What is it, Maggie?' he asked.

'Oh nothing,' I sighed. 'Just one of Mary's hairclips at the bottom of my bag.'

'You miss them, don't you?' asked Graham gently.

'Yes.' I nodded, trying to keep my voice steady. 'An awful lot. But hopefully Louisa and I will be able to pop round and see them soon.'

As the weeks passed, I kept myself busy. I knew I wasn't allowed to contact Gillian or Adrian and I didn't hear another peep from them.

Just over a month after the children had gone, Becky came round to see me.

'How are you doing?' she asked. 'Are you keeping busy?'

'Yes,' I told her. 'I've been doing a bit of pottering. I even sorted out the garden for spring the other day and if you want to know anything about wedding flowers and bridesmaid dresses then I'm your woman.'

'It sounds like Louisa has been keeping you busy,' she laughed.

'So are you ready to take on some new placements yet? Just say the word and I'll put you straight back on the available list.'

I shook my head.

'Not just yet, Becky, I'm sorry.'

'Maggie, I'm really worried about you,' she said, her eyes full of concern. 'In all of the years I've known you, you've never had a break this long. It's so unlike you not to want to have a new placement in. That's normally what keeps you going when children leave or go off for adoption.'

'I just feel like I'm not ready yet,' I lied.

'I've got a child coming into care in a couple of weeks who I think would be perfect for you,' she told me. 'It's a seven year-old boy. He's got autism and his mum is struggling to cope. It might just be a case of offering her some short-term respite so she can have a bit of a break or it could be something longer.

'What do you think?' asked Becky. 'I know you've fostered autistic children before and coped really well.'

I couldn't even look her in the eye as I answered.

'Becky, I can't. I just don't feel up to any new placements at the moment.'

'But why, Maggie?' she pressed me. 'What's stopping you?'

I looked at her and instinctively she knew exactly what I was thinking.

'I knew there was something going on,' she sighed. 'Maggie, you can't keep yourself free on the off chance that those children come back into the care system. For a start, you need to keep fostering to make a living, but more importantly, it's what you do. It's your vocation, it's what you're good at.

'We need you,' she urged. 'There are children that need you.'

'But what if the adoption breaks down?' I sighed. 'I feel responsible for those kids. I let them go even when I knew it wasn't right. I need to be there to help them if it goes wrong.'

'If is the right word. It's all ifs and buts. Hopefully that won't happen. Hopefully the children have settled down. You can't keep yourself free forever just on the off chance. It's madness, Maggie,' she told me firmly. 'It's been over a month and everything seems fine.'

'I know, I know,' I sighed.

I knew Becky was right. It was silly putting my life and fostering career on hold on the off chance things wouldn't work out. It had been over a month now. How long was I prepared to keep it up?

'If you're really that anxious about them, why don't you give Lisa a call?' she suggested.

I'd had the odd text from her reassuring me that everything was fine but we hadn't spoken. That afternoon I phoned her.

'I just wanted to give you a ring to see how Mary, Sean and Dougie were getting on,' I said lightly, desperately trying to keep my voice casual.

'Oh, fine,' she replied. 'I've been popping in a couple of times a week and everything seems OK. I think Sean's been a bit of a challenge but we expected that and Gillian and Adrian are coping.'

'I'm happy to hear that,' I sighed.

'Oh, Maggie, you're not still worrying that it's not going to work, are you? Honestly it all seems to be fine.

'You'll be able to see for yourself in a couple of weeks, anyway,' she continued. 'We said you'd visit after six weeks so I'll arrange for you and Louisa to pop in for a cup of tea.'

'That would be great, thanks,' I said. 'I'd really love that.'

I knew I had to accept what everyone was telling me. I'd never been so happy to have been proved wrong and for the first time in over a month, I felt some of the tension ebb away.

I rang Becky back.

'Put me down for that placement and any others that come up,' I told her decisively.

'That's the Maggie I know and love,' she laughed. 'It's good to have you back.'

I had to face facts. I'd been wrong. Becky was right, I couldn't keep myself free for ever and I had to move on with my life. There were other children that needed looking after and I knew it would do me good to immerse myself in caring for another child. But when seven weeks had passed and I still hadn't heard anything from Lisa about us visiting the children, I gave her another call.

'I'd really like to go and see the children,' I reminded her. 'It's important that Louisa and I don't just disappear from their lives and we did say six weeks when we had the planning meeting.'

'I'll give Adrian and Gillian a ring and try and organise something.' she replied. 'Leave it with me.'

She called me back the following day.

'I'm sorry, Maggie, they don't feel like it's a good time for you to go and visit,' she told me apologetically. 'Sean's still a bit up and down so they're worried it might upset him more to see you.'

I felt a sting of disappointment.

'You know as well as I do, Lisa, that sometimes seeing their foster carer actually settles children down,' I told her. 'It's reassurance for them that Louisa and I haven't just disappeared for ever.

'It doesn't have to be a whole day or even an hour,' I continued. 'All I'm asking for is a quick twenty-minute visit to pop in and see the children and say hello. I really think it would help.'

'I agree with you, Maggie,' sighed Lisa. 'I've discussed all that with Gillian and Adrian but unfortunately I have to go with what they decide and they don't think you seeing the children is a good idea at this point.'

I knew there was nothing I could do about it but I still felt sad. All along I'd promised the children that Louisa and I would visit them in their new house and I knew that it was terribly important to them. Their biological parents had gone without saying goodbye and it broke my heart that they might think I had done the same.

'Lisa, tell me the truth,' I urged her. 'Are Adrian and Gillian managing?'

She hesitated.

'I think so.'

'If either of them ever want to ring or text me, I'd be happy to help,' I went on.

'Thanks, Maggie, but I think they're working it out on their own,' she said.

As frustrating as it was, I had to put this behind me and try to move on. The following week I started sorting out the bedroom for the seven-year-old boy who was coming to stay with me. His name was Kai so I'd found a light-up letter 'K' in TK Maxx for his bedroom and I'd got out the toy castle and a few cars that I thought he might like. I was just making some space for his things in the chest of drawers when my mobile rang.

My heart leapt when I saw Lisa's number flash up on the screen. I hoped she was ringing to tell me when Louisa and I could visit the children.

'Hi, Lisa,' I said cheerfully. 'How are you?'

'Not good, Maggie,' she sighed.

I could tell by the tone of her voice that something awful had happened.

'What?' I asked, my heart in my throat. 'What is it?'

'I need your help, Maggie. It's urgent. I need you to pick up Sean, Dougie and Mary from their new school as soon as you can.'

'Today? Right now?' I asked, shocked. 'But why? Where are Gillian and Adrian?'

Lisa let out a long sigh.

'This morning Gillian and Adrian turned up at Social Services with the children's belongings. They said they'd had enough and they couldn't cope with them any more so the kids are back in the care system.

'Your gut feeling was right, Maggie. The adoption's well and truly broken down.'

SIXTEEN

Back to the Start

My head was spinning as I tried to take in what Lisa was telling me.

'I can't believe it,' I gasped. 'I thought everything was going OK. When did it happen? Do the children know?'

'Oh, Maggie, it's a complete and utter mess,' Lisa sighed.

She explained that Adrian and Gillian had taken the children to school as normal that morning.

'The next thing we knew a pile of boxes and cases was left in Social Service's reception and they told my colleague the children would need picking up from school at 3.20 p.m. because they didn't want them back.'

I couldn't believe what I was hearing. Even though I'd had my doubts about them, to abandon the children in such a callous way didn't sound like Gillian and Adrian.

I felt sick to my stomach at the thought of Sean, Mary and Dougie and all I could think about were how those poor kids were going to cope with yet another rejection. How on earth were we going to tell them?

'Maggie, please can you have them back?' begged Lisa. 'This is going to be devastating for them and I think it would help if they were somewhere familiar rather than having to go and live with complete strangers.'

'I'm so sorry, but I can't,' I sighed, desperately wishing otherwise. 'I've just agreed to foster a little boy and he's arriving next week.'

'Is there absolutely nothing you can do?' she pleaded. 'I'm just worried if there's no one who can take all three of them together, I'll have to split them up.'

I knew how disastrous it would be for the children to be separated from one another. I remembered how much comfort and security they all took from being close to each other.

'The only thing I can suggest is that you call my supervising social worker Becky and explain what's happened. Maybe there's something that she can do,' I told Lisa.

'OK,' she replied. 'I'll ring her right now and get straight back to you.'

As I put the phone down, I realised that my hands were shaking. It was such a shock. The thing that I'd dreaded happening the most had actually happened, and I felt sick at the knowledge that I'd been proven right.

Ten minutes later Becky phoned.

'Oh, Maggie,' she sighed. 'Lisa just called and told me what's going on. I'm so sorry.'

'Is there any way I can have the children back?' I asked her at once. 'Becky, they're going to be in such a state and I feel so responsible. I know I said yes to that other placement but could another foster carer take Kai? They really need me.'

'As I said to Lisa, I'm sure I can sort something out,' she reassured me. 'I'll find someone else to take him.'

'Oh, thank you so, so much,' I sighed gratefully.

This was the first time that I'd ever gone back on a placement and letting a child down wasn't something I did lightly.

'Lisa wants you to drive to the children's school where she'll meet you in the car park,' Becky told me. 'I'm just about to text you the address.

'Maggie, drive carefully,' she added. 'I really don't envy you having to do this. I hope the kids are OK.'

I knew they wouldn't be. How could they be? We were about to deliver the most heartbreaking news that their forever mummy and daddy, their brand new family, had changed their minds and didn't want them after all. They were facing yet more change in their little lives and being rejected for a second time.

I was also confused about how it had gone so drastically wrong with Gillian and Adrian that they couldn't manage them any more.

When I pulled up into the school car park, Lisa was sitting in her car waiting. She looked stressed and exhausted.

'Thanks for coming so quickly, I really appreciate it,' she told me.

'I honestly can't believe this is happening,' I sighed. 'I thought after two months things had settled down and they were going to be OK. Have you spoken to Gillian and Adrian?' I asked her.

'My colleague took the phone call this morning, then when I tried to call them back they wouldn't even answer the phone,' she replied. 'I've been tearing my hair out all day. In the end I went round to the house and eventually they let me in.'

Lisa explained that she had spent a couple of hours with them, talking to them about the difficulties they'd had and offering to put a plan together to offer them more support or put some respite care in place.

'They were having absolutely none of it,' she sighed. 'They're adamant that they don't want the children back. Gillian said looking after them had made her ill, it had put their marriage under strain and they simply couldn't cope.'

'But why didn't you tell me they were struggling?' I asked, frustrated.

'Honestly, Maggie, I had no idea things were so bad. Whenever I went round, Gillian said they were coping. You were right. You had your doubts and I should have listened to you. I'm so sorry, Maggie.'

'I'm sorry that I was right,' I sighed. 'I honestly didn't want this to happen. I'm heartbroken for the children. They're going to be so distraught.'

Lisa looked at her watch.

'The kids will be finishing school in ten minutes and expecting Gillian to pick them up. How on earth are we going to explain it to them, Maggie?' she sighed. 'How do we break the news that their forever family doesn't want them?'

'It's horrendous, and it's going to be a really tough conversation to have,' I told her. 'But I think we just have to bite the bullet and do it.'

Lisa had already warned the school about what was going on and all three children were in a classroom together with a teaching assistant.

I felt desperately sad and also terribly guilty that I'd been part of the process in building their excitement about their forever family. I couldn't believe that now, two months down the line, I was here helping to break the news that their new mummy and daddy didn't want them after all.

The school secretary showed us down the corridor.

'They're in here with the teaching assistant,' she said.

As we walked into the room, the first thing that hit me was the overpowering smell of faeces. Sean was lying on the floor, kicking a desk and I knew straight away that he had soiled himself. I was shocked to see that his lovely long hair had been cut into a severe short back and sides.

'Sean, get up please, your social worker needs to talk to you,' the TA told him firmly.

'F**k off,' he spat.

Dougie meanwhile was climbing up a pile of chairs in the corner of the room. Mary was the only one who noticed us as we came in as she was sitting quietly on a chair, fiddling with a pencil. Her mouth gaped open in surprise when she saw me.

'Why are you here?' she asked, her eyes wide with shock.

'Hello, lovey.' I smiled. 'Lisa and I have come to talk to you.'

As I looked around the room at these three children, my heart sank. It was like going back in time to the first day that I had met them.

The children weren't dirty but they looked unkempt. Mary's hair was lank and straggly and she didn't have any bobbles, bows or clips in it. They all had dark hollows under their eyes and the strain of the last couple of months on their little faces was plain to see.

'I think Sean might need taking to the toilet,' Lisa told the TA gently. 'Have you got a spare pair of pants and trousers?'

'Oh yes, I've got plenty.' She nodded.

'Does this happen a lot?' I asked her.

'Yep, several times a day,' she sighed wearily. 'We're used to it now.'

I was horrified to hear that he'd regressed so much with his toilet-training. While Sean was getting cleaned up, I tried to get Dougie to come and sit down but he wouldn't even acknowledge me.

He was still climbing his way up a stack of precariously balanced chairs.

'Dougie, that looks dangerous,' I pleaded with him. 'Come and sit down.'

He ignored me and started head-butting the chairs.

'Dougie,' said Lisa firmly. 'Stop that. You're going to hurt yourself, now come down please.'

As she reached out to lift him down, he sank his teeth into her arm.

'Ouch,' she yelled.

I lifted him off.

'You don't bite people, Dougie,' I told him firmly, putting him on the ground.

A few minutes later an angry-looking Sean came back from the toilet with the TA. As soon as they walked back in, he started running around the room. Dougie was now crawling around the floor underneath the desks. Neither of the boys had said a word to me or even acknowledged that I was there. It was as though I was invisible.

'How are we going to talk to these kids if they won't even sit still?' whispered Lisa.

I rummaged around in my handbag and dug out a

half-empty packet of fruit pastilles in the hope that sucking one would help calm them down.

'Right, who wants a sweet?' I asked. 'You can only have one if you sit on a chair.'

At the mention of sweets, Dougie ran over to me. Sean tried to grab one.

'Not until you sit down,' I told him.

They both sat down reluctantly, and I handed them one.

'Now suck your sweet while Lisa talks to you. Mary, would you like one too?'

To my surprise, she shook her head, refusing to even look at me.

Lisa took a deep breath and cleared her throat. My heart was pounding out of my chest as she began to explain why we were there to collect them and not Gillian.

'Adrian and Gillian are finding things very difficult at the moment,' she explained gently. 'So they've asked if you can go and live with Maggie for a while.'

I noticed that she'd referred to them by their names and not 'Mummy and Daddy' any more. It was important that she kept it open because at this point, we didn't really know what was happening with Gillian and Adrian and there was a chance they might decide to rethink their decision. For all we knew it was something that could be resolved when they'd had time and space to think it over.

'Did you all hear what Lisa was telling you?' I asked them. 'You're going to be coming back to my house with me.'

Sean and Dougie looked at me blankly and were more interested in eating their sweets.

'So Gillian and Adrian don't want us any more then?' asked Mary matter-of-factly.

'It's not about them not wanting you any more, lovey,' I told her gently. 'It's about them not being able to manage things at the moment.'

She turned to Sean.

'It's all your fault,' she spat. 'It's cos of you they don't want us.'

Sean got up and pushed his chair over.

'Well I didn't f***ng like them anyway,' he shouted. 'They were horrible.'

Then he grabbed Dougie, pulling him to the floor as the two of them began rolling around, play-fighting.

I could tell the boys weren't really listening and hadn't fully understood what Lisa was telling them. In a way it didn't matter. All they needed to know at this point was that they were coming back to my house. The questions could come later.

'Maggie, can I have a quiet word outside?' Lisa asked me.

We left the TA to deal with the chaos that was unfolding inside the classroom. As we walked out into the corridor, I gave a heavy sigh and stifled a sob in my throat. I felt such an overwhelming sense of sadness for them.

'It's heartbreaking to see them like that,' I sniffed. 'They've regressed to how they were all those months ago when they first came to me.'

The boys were wild; they were snarling and angry and wouldn't keep still. Mary was quiet and refused to even look at me.

'Lisa, how can you have not seen that this was happening?' I asked her, frustrated.

'I can only go by what people tell me on the phone and what I see with my own eyes, Maggie,' she sighed. 'I knew they'd had a few ups and downs. The kids seemed OK when I went round. They didn't say much when I spoke to them but it's only today that I realised things had got this bad. I'm as distressed as you are, Maggie.'

I knew there was no use in pointing the finger or trying to put the blame on anyone. Lisa would have done what she could, but the sad reality was, social workers are incredibly stressed and overworked. They don't have time to visit children frequently and spend hours with them. Lisa had checked in when she could and had believed what Gillian and Adrian had been telling her.

'We can talk about what went wrong until the cows come home but what we need to do now is get these children back to my house,' I told her firmly.

I hoped that if they went somewhere familiar to them, it would help settle them down.

'I'll see you back there,' Lisa told me apologetically.

She was going to pick up the children's things from Social Services and bring them back.

Even getting them into the car was a nightmare. Mary was fine but the boys were leaping around, whacking each other and refusing to sit in their car seats.

I lifted Dougie into his car seat and he struggled and kicked and pulled my hair.

'No,' he screamed. 'I don't want to.'

It was well over an hour's drive back to my house and if they were behaving like this, I wasn't sure how on earth I was going to manage.

'Oh my goodness, look at the time,' I exclaimed in a bright voice. 'It's nearly teatime. Let's get our seat belts on and I'll see if we can stop at McDonald's on the way back to my house. 'We'll have a drive-thru. How about that then?'

I would have tried any trick in the book to get them calmly and safely strapped in the car.

'Yay!' said Dougie, leaping into his car seat.

'I don't want anything,' Mary growled sullenly.

'You just have a drink then,' I told her.

I found the nearest McDonald's and they ate their burgers as I drove. To my relief, that kept them calm and quiet. As I drove, my brain was whirring. I couldn't believe how different they all were from the last time I'd seen them. What on earth had happened over the last eight weeks?

After what seemed like forever, I finally pulled up outside my house.

'This is where we lived with you!' shouted Dougie.

'Yes, and you're going to live here with me again for a little bit.' I smiled, relieved that he remembered.

'Is my bedroom still there?' asked Sean.

'Well, when we go in you can go and have a look,' I told him.

As I opened the front door, Louisa wandered out of the living room into the hallway. She had a look of absolute shock on her face when she saw the children.

'Er – what the . . .?' she gasped.

'Oh, hi, Louisa,' I said loudly. 'Look who's come back to stay with us for a while.

'I'm so sorry, I didn't have chance to ring you,' I muttered under my breath. 'I'll explain later.'

Lisa arrived on the doorstep a few minutes later.

'Louisa, would you mind sorting out Mary with a bowl of cereal because she didn't fancy a McDonald's earlier,' I asked her. 'And the boys might want some juice and a biscuit.'

I wanted them out of the way so Lisa could bring their things in. As I helped her carry box after box into the hallway, I realised this wasn't just a few of their possessions, this was everything they owned in its entirety.

'Come on,' I told her when we'd finished. 'I think we could both do with a cuppa.'

We went into the kitchen to put the kettle on. Mary was sitting at the table, Dougie was running around the room with a biscuit in his mouth and Sean was sitting on the floor.

I was getting a couple of mugs out of the cupboard when Mary screamed.

'Sean, what on earth are you doing?' shouted Louisa.

Lisa and I turned around just in time to see him stand on the table, pull down his trousers and wee all over the plate of biscuits.

Lisa's mouth gaped open in horror.

'No, Sean!' yelled Mary. 'That's disgusting.'

I went over to him.

'Get down now, Sean,' I told him firmly, offering him a hand to help him down. 'We wee in the toilets in this house. Did you forget?'

'Don't want to,' he said, giving me a sly smile.

'Let's get this cleaned up,' I sighed.

Louisa and Lisa were horrified but I knew there was no point in getting cross. I cleared everything off the table, mopped up the puddle of urine with kitchen roll and wiped it down with disinfectant.

I couldn't be angry with Sean because I knew it was his anxiety coming out. He didn't know what was going on or what was happening and he felt out of control. Him weeing on the table was his way of trying to take back some control.

'That's what he did at Gillian and Adrian's house,' sighed Mary. 'Gillian was really cross and kept sending him to his bedroom but he wouldn't stay there.'

'Oh dear,' I told her. 'It sounds like things have been very difficult.'

Part of me was desperate to ask her more questions to try and find out what had gone on, but she'd been through enough and I knew that she'd tell me in her own time.

After an hour Lisa left.

'Good luck, Maggie,' she said to me sympathetically. 'I hope they and you manage to get some sleep and I'll give you a ring tomorrow to see how things are.

'What a horrendous day,' she sighed and I nodded sadly.

The rest of the evening was like déjà vu. The boys trashed the room, getting out every toy, throwing around Lego and smashing up the models they'd built when they were with me before. Mary was sullen and silent.

Bedtime took hours, with the boys refusing to put on their pyjamas, climbing the furniture and repeatedly getting out of bed. By the time all three of them were finally in bed, I was exhausted. I flopped down on the sofa beside Louisa, my head in my hands.

'What on earth happened, Maggie?' she asked, looking concerned. 'Why have they come back? What's happened to Gillian and Adrian?'

'I don't know the whole story yet, but I just don't think they could cope with the reality of three damaged children,' I sighed.

When they move to a new home, children will often push the boundaries at first. Insecurity will mean that they revert to behaviours that are familiar, and for these three that meant retreating to the safety of their wild behaviour.

The longer they went on without suitable boundaries or displays of love and affection, the children would have been in a constant state of fight or flight. For the majority of their short lives, normality had been running wild, going to bed when and where they could and going to the toilet wherever they wanted. So when things got tough, it was unsurprising that they'd go back to those routines. That sort of disruptive behaviour was their security blanket and whenever they were faced with fear or insecurity they'd revert completely.

'But how come they got so bad?' sighed Louisa. 'They haven't even been gone that long.'

I shook my head sadly.

'It's horrible to see, but kids can regress in a matter of weeks.'

'I feel so sorry for them,' Louisa told me, her voice trembling.

'I know, lovey,' I said, wrapping my arms around her. 'We all do. They're going to need a lot of love and patience to get them through this but I promise we will do it.'

Before I went to bed, I went to check on the children. The boys thankfully had passed out at long last, completely exhausted. But when I went into Mary's room she was lying there wide awake, staring at the ceiling. I went and sat on her bed.

'Are you OK, flower?' I asked her gently. 'You haven't said a word to me since we've got back.'

Her eyes filled with angry tears but she refused to look at me.

'I'm not talking to you cos you're a liar,' she spat. 'You said they were our new mummy and daddy. You said they were our forever family but they're not. They didn't want us, did they?'

I tried to take her hand but she shrugged me off.

'I'm so sorry, lovey,' I told her. 'I so wanted it to be OK. That's what we all wanted. We desperately wanted them to be your forever family but sometimes things don't work out the way that we want them to. We thought they were the right mummy and daddy for you, but they weren't and I'm so very sorry for that, flower.'

Mary turned her back to me, curling up into a tight ball and I knew there was nothing more that I could say.

I kissed her head gently and left the room with a heavy heart.

Would these poor children ever trust anyone again?

SEVENTEEN

Déjà vu

Even if I had to start right from the beginning, I was determined to get these children back to where they had been before they'd left my house.

All I could do was put the same strict routine and rules in place and hope that it had the same effect as before. Of course, it was hugely demoralising when I was cleaning poo off the floor for the third time that day, and it was exhausting having to pull them off furniture and sit outside their bedrooms for hours at night to make sure they stayed in bed but I knew I had no other option.

I had to go back to how things were when they first came, in the hope that it would give them the safety and security they so desperately needed. I locked rooms from the inside so they couldn't go rampaging around the house, I removed anything that could be swung off or thrown from their bedrooms and started setting the alarm on my phone again to take them to the toilet. Time after time I carried them back to the table in a bid to get them to sit down to eat and I was constantly reminding them to use a knife and fork rather than their hands. If they didn't, I took the food away.

'I think Sean's finished his dinner now,' I told Louisa if he started messing about.

The first couple of days were desperate times and the boys were so wild and out of control that I resorted to ice pops or lollipops to calm them when they were having a meltdown.

One morning Sean ran into the kitchen and started pulling all of the toys out of the cupboard.

'Where's the f****ing Lego?' he shouted.

'Sean, lovey, remember that we don't swear in this house,' I told him calmly.

'But where's the Lego?' he yelled.

'I've taken the Lego away and I'll bring it back out when I know that you can sit quietly and play with it rather than throwing it or smashing it. Can you remember that's what I did before when you first came to live with me?'

'I f****ng hate you, Maggie!' he shouted.

He was so angry all the time, far more than he'd ever been when he first arrived.

School was out of the question for the moment, but I tried to get them all to do simple activities like playing with Play-Doh and printing with potatoes to get them used to sitting and concentrating again. I wanted to jog their memory and remind them of things that we'd done before and get them ready to go back to their old school. Unfortunately the boys had regressed so much they were finding it impossible to sit for any length of time.

'If you can't sit still at the table, then we won't do them,' I told Dougie. 'It's as simple as that.'

Life was rigid, routine-based and frankly joyless, but I knew I had to keep persevering.

Lisa came round after a couple of days to check how things were going.

'How are the kids coping?' she asked.

I shrugged.

'Understandably, Mary's very hurt and angry and she's blaming me,' I told her. 'The boys are so wild and disruptive that the sadness hasn't come yet, but I'm sure it will.'

Lisa explained that she had been round to see Gillian and Adrian again.

'They were a lot calmer but nothing's changed. It's as we thought. The children regressed to the same behaviours that they had when they came to you and they simply weren't able to cope. Sean and Dougie were going to the toilet everywhere, simulating sex with each other and swearing. They were destructive and disruptive and it was just way too much for them.'

'There's no way around it, it's hell,' I sighed. 'Anyone would struggle. I've been there and I'm living it again now. But the only way to get through it is to stick it out and hope that those behaviours will eventually change. I just wish they'd asked for help before it was too late.'

'Unfortunately, Gillian and Adrian weren't prepared to see it through,' replied Lisa. 'I don't think they were able to attach to the children and in turn the children didn't attach to them. To be honest, even if they said they'd changed their minds and wanted the children back I wouldn't take them. It's gone too far for that. It's clear to me now that they're not the right parents for these children and I just wish I'd seen it sooner. They can't manage them and I couldn't do that to these kids again.'

It was a relief for me to hear that.

'You were right to be unsure about this adoption,' she sighed. 'If only I had listened to your concerns in the first place.'

'I honestly never wanted this to happen,' I told her. 'For the children's sake I desperately wanted it to work. I'm not taking any sense of satisfaction from any of this.'

'Gosh, Maggie, I know you're not,' she sighed.

Lisa also explained that she had spoken to the school that they'd been going to.

'Sean has been in isolation pretty much from day one and was on the verge of being expelled,' she said. 'Surprisingly, Mary and Dougie had both been very disruptive too. Mary's gone backwards in her reading and literacy.'

We decided to give them a full week at home with me to try and adjust before they went back to their old school. In the meantime I gave Mrs Moody a ring to try and sort out places for them.

'It's good to hear from you, Maggie,' she said. 'Have you got a new foster child in already?'

'No, sadly I haven't,' I said. 'I'm ringing about Mary, Sean and Dougie. I'm afraid the children's adoption has broken down and they're back living with me.'

'Oh no, Maggie, I'm so sorry to hear that,' she sighed. 'I'm devastated for them. How are they?'

'Not great,' I replied. 'But I think going back to school will help settle them down.'

'Well you know we'd be happy to have them back whenever you feel they're ready,' she assured me. 'It will probably take a couple of days as we'll need to sort out a teaching assistant who can do one-to-one with Sean.'

'He's definitely going to need that at first,' I said. 'I'm confident that if we all work together we can get them back to where they were.'

'Does this happen a lot?' she asked me suddenly, her voice filled with shock. 'Parents changing their minds about adopting children and giving them back?'

'Sadly it happens a lot with older children, yes,' I sighed.

As devastating as it was, the breakdown of an adoption wasn't a rare thing. The statistics show that six out of ten adoptions involving older children (over five years old) break down. It tends to happen less with little ones who are more adaptable and controllable and have less trauma and memory of their lives before they entered the care system.

'Has this ever happened to you before?' asked Mrs Moody.

'Only once, thank goodness, many years ago,' I told her.

In my entire fostering career I'd thankfully only ever had one other adoption break down. It was an eight-year-old girl called Molly who had ADHD. Sadly, her adoptive parents simply couldn't cope with her behaviour. They just weren't prepared for the toll a child with special needs was going to take on their lives.

When an adoption fails, it's a sad situation all round and it's not fair to apportion blame. It's not the children's fault and I always tried not to blame the adopters either. It's not easy to walk away from a little one and I know adopters feel a lot of shame and guilt when they give up on a child. They have to live with that decision for the rest of their lives.

They would have gone through a long process to become approved as adopters and no doubt would have told friends, family and work colleagues, who would be excited for them. To admit that you can't cope with a child would never be an easy decision. I was frustrated and annoyed that Gillian and Adrian had given up on these three children so soon, but I also knew deep down that it wasn't fair to blame them. I really did believe they wanted the best for the kids but sadly, despite their best efforts, it had all been too much. You can be warned about a child's behaviour but until you're living with it 24–7 you don't really know how you're going to cope.

Time is no guarantee of success either. While some adoptions break down after weeks or months, some break down even years later. I've fostered a child whose adoption broke down after eight years of living with a couple who'd looked after her since she was five years old. She became a teenager, went off the rails and her adoptive parents simply couldn't manage her behaviour any more and she went back into care.

I knew the events of the last few days had all come as a real shock to Louisa too. Since she'd come to live with me I'd fostered lots of children who had gone on to be adopted and thankfully they'd all worked out. She'd never even considered the fact they might not work and I knew she found it really upsetting that the children had been handed back.

'When will they be adopted again?' she asked me. 'When will Lisa start looking for new parents for them? I hope she makes a better job of it this time.'

She was so desperate for them to have their happy ending.

'Sweetie, the sad thing is they probably won't,' I sighed. 'Because of their age, it's unlikely Social Services will put them up for adoption again.'

'So they only get one chance?' she gasped, tears in her eyes. 'But that's so unfair.'

'It's not about having only one chance,' I explained gently. 'It's about what's right for each child and the reasons why the previous adoption broke down.'

'It's not the children's fault that Lisa picked the wrong mum and dad,' she huffed.

'It's just the system unfortunately,' I told her. 'It could be that long-term fostering is the best thing for them now.'

Carol was another person who was devastated to hear that the adoption had broken down and she rang me every couple of days to see how the children were.

'I'm so sad for them,' she told me. 'Let me know if I can come round and see them.'

After they'd been back with me for a week she came round to visit.

As she walked into the kitchen Dougie and Sean were wrestling on the floor.

'Oh, boys,' she exclaimed, beaming at them. 'It's so lovely to see you. I've missed you.'

But neither of them said a word to her. They barely glanced at her before jumping up and running around the room.

'Gosh, I didn't expect them to be this bad,' she told me quietly, as we watched the boys play-fighting on the floor. 'They won't even acknowledge me.'

'I'm so choked up for them that they didn't get their happy ending,' she sighed and I could see tears in her eyes.

'Where's Mary?' she asked.

'She's upstairs reading,' I told her. 'It's like she's gone into herself. She's quiet and sullen and very angry. She blames me.'

Carol shook her head sadly.

'Oh, Maggie, I'm so sorry that things have worked out like this,'

'I must admit this week has been really hard,' I sighed. 'I feel like I'm back to square one again.'

'You're doing an amazing job,' she assured me.

I honestly didn't feel like I was. For a start I was absolutely exhausted. The boys were waking up at 5 a.m. and banging around in their bedroom so I was forced to take them downstairs so they didn't wake up Mary or Louisa.

'Right, let's sit and watch some cartoons,' I told them one morning. 'I'll get the iPad.'

But both of them completely ignored me. Dougie was climbing on the back of the sofa and jumping off and Sean had pulled his pyjamas down and was weeing all over the rug.

I'd reached the end of my tether. I collapsed on a chair at the kitchen table and buried my head in my hands. The boys were throwing plastic beakers at each other now and I was honestly too tired to stop them.

'Maggie, are you OK?' said a voice from the doorway.

It was Louisa standing in her dressing gown. She went over to the boys and grabbed the beakers from them.

'Boys, you need to sit down and watch a cartoon,' she told them firmly.

She put on the iPad on and soon they were glued to CBBC. Then she mopped up the puddle of wee.

'I'm sorry,' I sighed. 'I just couldn't do it. I've reached my limit. I think the past week is catching up with me and I'm shattered.'

'It's OK,' she said. 'I know it's hard work.'

'It's so demoralising to see them like this,' I told her. 'I worked so hard last time to give them structure and routine and make them feel secure but now it's like that never happened.'

It was relentless but I knew there was no other option than to carry on. A couple of weeks after they'd returned to my house, the children started school again. Although I was worried about how they would cope, much to my relief it seemed to help. Their teachers had explained what had happened to their classmates so they didn't ask too many upsetting questions and all three of the children seemed genuinely delighted to see their teachers and old friends. Sean was still very unsettled and had good and bad days, but his amazing TA was extremely patient with him.

After a couple of weeks I realised that things had started to improve. The boys were slightly calmer and I'd allowed them to have a few of the toys back. I was getting clean underpants from Dougie, and Sean wasn't pooing and weeing wherever he liked, although I was still having to use the timer with him.

It went off one afternoon while he was playing with the train track.

'Sean, time to go to the toilet,' I told him.

'Not this again,' he groaned.

'It will only stop when you're prepared to use the toilet properly,' I explained.

'I am doing it properly!' he shouted.

'Well you need to show me that then,' I told him gently.

I agreed to turn off the timer and for the rest of the day he managed to use the toilet and stay dry.

It was only a little thing but it was a significant step in the right direction.

But once the wildness had started to calm down, the anger and the upset followed as the boys started to process what had happened to them.

At last, I'd allowed them to have the Lego back and one morning Dougie was playing with it in the kitchen.

'I once builded Lego with my new daddy, didn't I, Maggie?' he said wistfully.

'You did, lovey.' I smiled sadly. 'When he first met you at this house you built some lovely models together. Did you build Lego with him at your new house?'

Dougie shook his head.

'Sean smashed up all the models and Gillian said we made too much of a mess so she took it away.'

I couldn't criticise her for that as I had done the same when they'd moved in with me initially.

'Maggie, why didn't our new mummy and daddy like us?' he asked, staring up at me with his big blue eyes.

My heart broke for him.

'It's not that they didn't like you, sweetie,' I promised him. 'They really liked you. They wanted you to go and live with them, remember? I think they just found it hard because they'd never had children living with them before. They thought they could manage but they couldn't.'

I went over and wrapped my arms around him and gave him a cuddle.

'Maggie, are you going to send us away again soon?' he asked.

'What do you mean, flower?'

'Are we going back to Gillian and Adrian's when they're ready?'

I knew I couldn't lie to him. As painful as it was, I had to tell him the truth.

'I don't think you're going to go back to them, I'm afraid, Dougie,' I told him.

He snuggled in closer, and seemed to be processing everything.

'I did like Adrian, but I like it better here,' he said decisively after a moment, going back to playing with his Lego model.

It appeared to be preying on Sean's mind too. One night he appeared by my bed, shivering and soaked to the skin having wet the bed. He was crying too.

'We're not going back there, are we?' he mumbled, his teeth chattering. 'I don't want to go back there.'

'Go back where, flower?' I asked, rubbing my eyes, confused.

'To Gillian and Adrian's,' he whispered.

I could see he was drowsy but he looked terrified.

'No, sweetie. You're safe here now, I promise.'

I knew Lisa needed to come round and have another word with the children as they were getting very anxious. She came to talk to them that night.

'We've had a meeting and we've decided that you're not going to go back and live with Gillian and Adrian,' she told them.

I paused and waited for their reaction. The boys were unusually calm and I could see the relief on their faces.

'But where *are* we going?' asked Mary anxiously.

'Well, at this moment there are no plans for you to go anywhere,' Lisa told her. 'For the time being you're staying here with Maggie and if that changes we'll tell you.'

I hoped that would be enough to reassure them and help them settle.

Sean was still very angry about everything that had happened. One afternoon Carol offered to take Mary and Dougie out while I baked some bread with him.

'When I'm feeling really cross I like to knead the dough and then I slam it on the work surface,' I explained.

I gave him a quick demonstration and handed it to him.

'Your turn.' I smiled.

He pummelled the dough, kneading it again and again.

'So how are you feeling about not living with Gillian and Adrian any more?' I asked him, as I got to work on another ball of dough.

Sean slammed the bread dough hard against the work surface.

'I didn't like it,' he muttered. 'She didn't like me. She said I was dirty.'

I let him talk at the same time as kneading the bread.

'I did try. But even when I tried they didn't seem to notice. I hated it there anyway. I hated them.'

As he threw the dough down on the work surface, tears streamed down his face.

I went over to him and he buried his head into my shoulder. His body shook with huge gulping sobs.

'W-what did I do wrong?' he wept. 'Why didn't they want me, Maggie?'

'You did nothing wrong, lovey,' I soothed. 'It's not your fault.

'They weren't the right mummy and daddy for you. We thought they were, but we got it wrong and I'm so, so sorry.'

I held him close while he cried his eyes out.

'It's OK,' I whispered, ruffling his short hair. 'Everything's going to be OK.'

In my heart I truly hoped that it would be.

EIGHTEEN

A Good Idea

As the weeks passed, the children slowly started to settle down again. After finally letting out some of his feelings, Sean seemed more mellow and calm somehow. He was able to verbalise his anger far more and talk things through with me when he felt cross.

They'd been back with me for six weeks when Lisa came to see me one day.

'We really need to start thinking about what's going to happen to the children in the future,' she told me.

She paused and I knew exactly what she was going to say.

'Maggie, would you consider fostering them long term?' she asked. 'I know they're happy here and you're extremely fond of them.'

'I am,' I sighed. 'However, I would really need to think about it.'

'Take all the time you need.' She smiled.

I had grown to love these children. However, my big concern was that if I did foster the three of them long term

I wouldn't be able to foster any other children for the next ten years or so. The part of my job I loved the most was the variety and helping lots of different children.

I didn't know what to do and I spoke to Becky about it.

'My head is telling me I don't want to stop fostering,' I said. 'And even though I'm a massive advocate for single parents, I can't shake the niggling feeling that these three would really thrive from being with a two-parent family.'

I still felt that Sean and Dougie would benefit hugely from having a positive male role model as they were growing up.

'What's your heart telling you?' asked Becky.

'It's telling me that I love these children, they're happy with me and I can't risk them going to someone else and ending up being rejected again.'

They'd been through so much rejection and change, my heart broke at the thought they'd have to go through any more or even have to be split up if Social Services couldn't find one carer to take them all on.

'Maggie, I can't make that decision for you,' Becky told me. 'Only you can decide what you feel is best both for you and the children. If you agree to foster them long term, it is a big commitment so you have to be sure.'

I was in complete turmoil about it. When Carol popped round for a coffee one morning she could tell there was something on my mind.

'Are you OK, Maggie?' she asked. 'You seem distracted.'

'I'm sorry,' I sighed. 'Lisa has asked me if I want to foster the children permanently and I don't know what to do.'

I shared my concerns with her.

'What if you knew they were going to be fostered by someone who wasn't going to give up on them?' asked Carol. 'Someone who already knew these kids and their challenges.'

'Then I'd be delighted,' I said. 'That's the ideal scenario but unfortunately it doesn't exist.'

'It does,' said Carol, suddenly serious. 'Do you think Social Services would consider me as their long-term foster carer?'

'You?' I gasped with a mixture of shock and delight. 'But honestly, would you really want that? You know the challenges I've had. Would you really be prepared to take on all three of them?'

'Yes,' she said. 'I really would. You know how much I think of those kids and I feel like Sean and I really understand each other.'

I was still in shock.

'But what about your husband and son?' I asked. 'And you've already got a placement. Do you have room for all three of them?'

'Keiran's nearly eighteen so he'll be leaving the care system soon. Social Services are sorting him out with his own flat, so it won't be long until he moves out,' she explained. 'And my son Liam is busy with catering college and his friends, so he's barely in the house any more.

'I'd have to talk to Dave of course, but he's not keen on children coming and going. He prefers us to have long-term placements.'

I couldn't believe what I was hearing – it seemed like the ideal solution.

'I think I could give them the stability and the security they need and build on all the good work that you've done.' Carol smiled.

'I think it's a brilliant idea,' I told her, beaming. 'Talk to Dave and if you're both keen then let Becky know.'

Becky was the supervising social worker for both of us.

She rang me a few days later.

'Carol's been in touch and explained her idea. What do you feel about the idea of her fostering the children long term?'

'I was flabbergasted when she first told me,' I laughed. 'But once the shock wore off, I couldn't think of anywhere better for them to go and I'm behind her one hundred per cent.

'She knows the children,' I added. 'Our main struggle has always been Sean but the two of them have a lovely relationship and always have had since day one.'

I knew I would be sad to let the children go, but this way they would be going to someone I knew and trusted who they already had a relationship with. Carol was someone who had become a friend to me over the last few months and she was a genuine, lovely person who I knew wanted only the best for these kids.

Becky contacted Lisa and to let her know what we were thinking and she spoke to her manager. Then we all gathered for a meeting at Social Services the following week.

I could see Carol was nervous.

'What if they say no, Maggie?' she asked, biting her lip.

'They won't,' I assured her.

We all settled down with cups of tea, and I couldn't help but think how different this felt from the first time I'd met Gillian and Adrian to talk about the adoption.

'We've had a chat about Sean, Dougie and Mary coming to live with you in the long term, Carol, and we think that it could be a possibility,' Lisa explained. 'But bearing in mind what these children have been through, we need to make sure we get the timing right and work out the best way for the introductions to be done.'

My belief was that we had to do things very differently this time. There could be no talk of mummies and daddies and forever families.

'I think what we've got to do first is make sure the kids are comfortable with it and it's what they want,' I suggested. 'So rather than telling them this is what's going to happen, perhaps Carol could present the idea to them and ask their permission to explore it further?'

'It's a very different way to how we normally do things but I don't see why not,' said Lisa.

I felt that by doing it this way it would allow the children to feel as if they had more control. It would feel like they were making the decision about who they lived with rather than being told.

'That sounds good,' said Carol. 'But what if they turn around and say no?'

'I'm confident they won't.' I smiled. 'They know you already and they like you.'

The children didn't know Carol's husband Dave or her son Liam though, and they'd never been to her house. Lisa expressed her concerns about this.

'Why don't we slow all this down,' suggested Becky. 'Carol, how about you invite everyone round to your house so that the kids can meet Dave and Liam a few times? Then, if everyone is still in agreement, Carol can bring up the idea with the children.'

'I think that's a great idea,' I said.

I didn't want to rush things either. The children were still adjusting to life back at my house after the adoption had failed and I didn't want them to feel like they were being pushed on to the next place.

We arranged that Carol would invite us to her house the following weekend.

'Carol said it's not fair that she's always coming round here and she'd really like to invite us to her house so she's going to make us Sunday lunch,' I told the children.

'Will there be Yorkshire pudding?' asked Dougie, his eyes lighting up.

'Well, Carol's son Liam is training to be a chef so you never know.' I smiled.

The children didn't bat an eyelid but I could see Louisa was suspicious.

'Why are we going to Carol's?' she asked me that night when the children had gone to bed.

'She's my friend and I just thought it would be nice for a change,' I told her, trying to sound as innocent as I could. I could see she wasn't convinced though.

'You're plotting something, Maggie,' she said.

'Who me? Never!'

As the weekend drew closer, I prayed that the children would behave as I didn't want Dave to be put off. I needn't have worried. He was a big, tall man with a shock of red hair – the sort of bloke that you'd describe as a gentle giant. He seemed very calm and softly spoken. Liam was a polite lad who looked just like his dad. I could see Carol was nervous about how everyone was going to get along and what her husband and son would make of the kids.

'This is lovely,' I exclaimed as we all tucked into roast chicken with all the trimmings.

'Liam did it all,' said Carol proudly. 'He's at catering college and when he finishes he wants to be a professional chef.'

For once the children behaved brilliantly. When they started to get fidgety at the table Liam took Dougie into the living room to play FIFA on his PlayStation and Dave took Sean up to the loft to show him his telescope. While Louisa and I cleared the dishes away, Carol painted Mary's nails.

When Sean came back down, he looked impressed.

'The telescope's brilliant,' he told me. 'Dave said at night he can see all the stars and even the Milky Way.'

'Wow, that sounds amazing.' I smiled.

That evening, after I'd taken the kids home and got them to bed, Carol rang.

'Well, what did they think?' I asked nervously.

'Dave loved them,' she said, sounding excited. 'He's happy for us to go for it. He found Sean really interesting and they had a good chat about space.

'Don't worry, Maggie, we both know it's going to be a big change and a lot of hard work but we want to do it,' she added.

'I promise you we won't let the kids down. I couldn't do that to them again after everything they've been through.'

I was still keen not to rush things though.

'That's great,' I said. 'But let's sit with it for a bit and perhaps you and Dave can spend a little more time with the children together.'

So we came up with a plan. One Saturday Carol and Dave knocked at our door.

'Maggie, you don't have any spare children that we could borrow, do you? We really fancy going to the zoo today, but we've got nobody to go with,' Carol asked loudly.

'Me!' Dougie grinned, running out into the hall. 'I can come.'

'I want to come too,' said Sean.

'And me, and me,' Mary exclaimed.

'Are you sure?' I asked and all three of them nodded eagerly.

I made the most of a rare Saturday to myself, and Graham and I had a lovely walk together.

When the children came back that evening, Sean was in his element.

'There was a butterfly house there,' he told me excitedly. 'Dave knows all the names of them like me. He likes butterflies too.'

All three of them were full of beans, and I couldn't help but smile seeing them all looking so content.

'It sounds like you had a lovely day,' I said to Carol when she rang.

'We did, Maggie,' she sighed happily. 'The kids were great. We're both one hundred per cent sure we want this.'

'Well, why don't you give Lisa a ring in the morning and let's get the wheels in motion,' I told her.

The children had been back with me for two months and slowly they had settled back into life. The good thing was, because Carol only lived around the corner, they would still be able to go to the same school and they could see Louisa and me as often as they liked.

Lisa was being very cautious this time and I could see she was nervous about making another mistake.

'What if the children go back to their old behaviours that you have worked so hard to change?' she asked me. 'Do you think Carol will be able to cope with that?'

'Carol's an experienced foster carer,' I told her. 'She understands that they might regress but the difference is, unlike Gillian and Adrian, she knows how to manage it.'

Now Carol and I just needed to tell the children our idea and ask them what they thought.

'Are you sure you want to do it this way?' Lisa asked her. 'There's always the risk it will backfire.'

'It's a risk that I'm prepared to take,' Carol replied firmly. 'Maggie's right. I want them to want this too. I don't want them to feel like they're being forced into it.'

I agreed that it was important to make sure things were very different to how the adoption was last time.

I arranged for Carol and Dave to come round one night after school for tea. I was sure the children were going to like the idea, but the three of them had been through so many changes and there were no guarantees.

After we'd all eaten, Carol pushed her plate away and cleared her throat.

'Mary, Sean and Dougie, there's something Dave and I wanted to talk to you about,' she told them.

I could hear her voice quivering with nerves and Dave grabbed her hand and gave it a reassuring squeeze.

'We're both really fond of the three of you and have really enjoyed spending more time with you all. We wondered if you'd like to come and live with us?'

'What, at your house?' Dougie asked, his eyes wide.

'Yes, at our house.' Dave nodded.

'You could keep on going to the same school and you could come and see Maggie and Louisa whenever you wanted, but you would live at our house with me, Dave and Liam,' Carol explained.

'Just for a little while?' asked Sean, looking cautious.

'No, not for a little while. We'd like you to come and live with us for a long, long time, if you want to,' she said. 'For ever, in fact.'

'We want our house to be your home.'

She paused and looked at the children.

'So?' she asked nervously. 'What do you think?'

Three blank faces stared back at us. I'd never seen the children so quiet.

'Well?' I asked them. 'What do you think? Do you like the idea of going to live with Carol?'

'Yeah, I think that would be OK,' said Dougie. 'You've got more bedrooms than Maggie so will we get one each cos I don't want to share with Sean any more?'

We all laughed.

'I think we can probably manage that,' Carol told him.

'But, Maggie, is it OK if we leave your house?' asked Sean, looking worried. 'Do you mind if we go and live with Carol?'

'That's absolutely fine with me.' I beamed. 'I would be delighted if you were living with Carol and Dave because I know you would be really, really happy there and you'd be just around the corner.'

'What do you think, Mary?' I asked her.

Out of the three of them she had been the quietest.

'I suppose that's OK.' She shrugged.

'Now you've decided that it's a good idea, shall we mention this to Lisa and see what she thinks?' I said.

'I hope she says yes,' said Sean.

'But what if she says no?' asked Dougie, a look of worry on his little face.

'I'm sure we can all persuade her,' smiled Carol.

I was so pleased and relieved that after everything they'd been through, the children had taken it so well, particularly Sean, who I knew had struggled more than the others. They were all so much more enthusiastic than they'd ever been with Gillian and Adrian, and for the first time in months, I felt hopeful. Maybe finally things really were going to work out.

NINETEEN

Finding Forever

The boys seemed really excited about going to live with Carol, but it was Mary that I was worried about. That night I went into her bedroom to say goodnight.

'You've been very quiet, lovey,' I told her. 'How are you feeling about what Carol said earlier?'

She wouldn't look at me and I could tell that she was close to tears.

'How do we know she's not lying to us?' she asked angrily. 'How do you know she really likes us?'

'She's saying that she wants us to live with her forever but what if she changes her mind like Gillian and Adrian did?' she hissed. 'What's the point in going if she's just gonna send us back again?'

Her insecurities were totally understandable after everything that had happened.

I cupped her face in my hands.

'Sweetheart, Carol and Dave are not going to change their minds,' I promised her. 'They've thought long and hard about this and they want you to be part of their family.

'Carol knows you. She's seen all three of you at your worst and she still wants you to go and live with her. She's been a foster carer for years just like me. She knows some days are going to be good and some will be bad.

'It's not going to be like Adrian and Gillian,' I promised. 'They hadn't had children in their house before but Carol has so she knows exactly what it's like.'

Her anger seemed to fade away and she just looked terrified now.

'Mary, I know it's really hard because of last time but you just have to trust me on this,' I urged her.

All I could hope was that in time she'd believe me.

I rang Lisa the following morning.

'It went really well,' I told her. 'Mary had a bit of a wobble but I think it will be OK. Sean and Dougie are delighted but they want to ask your permission because they think it's their idea.'

'I'll pop over and see you all this afternoon then,' she said.

When Lisa came round, all three children were ready and waiting for her.

'Lisa, we've had a really good idea,' Sean told her. 'We want to go and live at Carol's house but we still want to stay at the same school and see Maggie. Could we do that?'

They waited nervously for her reply.

'Wow, you've got this all worked out, haven't you?' She smiled.

'Yes, and there's more bedrooms at Carol's house so we can have a bedroom each,' said Dougie.

Lisa laughed.

'I can see you've really thought this through,' she told him. 'But what does Carol say about this?'

'We asked Carol and she said it was a brilliant idea,' said Dougie.

'Well I had better have a chat with her then and try and get this sorted out,' she told them.

She looked over at me and gave me a knowing smile.

That night before I went to bed, I poked my head into the boys' room. Dougie was fast asleep but Sean was still awake.

'Get some sleep, mister,' I told him. 'It's late and you're going to be exhausted at school in the morning.'

I could see he was processing what had gone on today with Lisa.

'Maggie, do you really not mind if we go and live with Carol?' he asked me anxiously. 'Will you be sad?'

'I'll be a little bit sad because I'll miss you,' I told him. 'But you'll only be around the corner so I can see you lots.'

'Why aren't we staying here with you?' he asked, his eyes wide in the dark.

It was the question that I'd been dreading answering.

I went and sat on his bed.

'My job is to look after children until they find their forever family,' I explained gently. 'And the amazing thing is, you've found yours. Your forever is with Carol and Dave.'

'But what about Louisa?' he asked. 'She's stayed with you a very long time.'

'Ah yes, well I was Louisa's forever just like Carol is yours,' I told him, giving him a kiss on the top of his head.

Talking about Louisa had reminded me that I needed to tell her what was going on. She was staying at Charlie's for a couple of days so when she came back the following night I told her what was happening.

'So that was why you were being so weird,' she laughed. 'I thought it was strange when we went to Carol's for lunch and she kept coming round with her husband.'

'I didn't want to tell you until the children and Social Services had agreed and I knew it was definitely going to happen.' I smiled.

I could see from her face that she was disappointed, although she was trying to put on a brave face.

'What is it, lovey?' I asked. 'I thought you'd be happy for them.'

'I am,' she sighed. 'But why couldn't we keep them, Maggie? They're happy here.'

'They're lovely kids and I'm really fond of them and if nothing had worked out for them, then of course I'd have kept them,' I told her. 'But Carol's offered to foster them and it just feels right. You know I'm a great believer in fate and it feels like somehow this was meant to be. Plus it means that I can continue to foster a variety of children.'

'Maybe you're right,' she sighed.

Lisa agreed that we could start the handover straight away. To me it was crucial that this handover was done differently to the adoption that had broken down. As the children were going to live with someone they already knew and it was fostering rather than adoption, it could be a lot less formal and structured this time.

'You talk to Carol and do it however you feel is best,' Lisa told me.

One morning when the children were going off to school I told them: 'I'm going to drop some of your stuff round at Carol's house today. Perhaps after tea we can pop round and you can start to sort out your new bedrooms?'

Popping round to Carol's became something that we did every few days. It was just like going to a friend's house.

Sean was excited because Liam had given him his old bike that had been in the garage. One afternoon I stood at the end of Carol's road and let him cycle down the pavement to her house.

Sean would ask to go round there himself. I'd walk him round and he'd stay for tea and Liam would walk him back later on. It was lovely to see that he really wanted to be there.

There was no awkwardness this time and it felt natural and easy – the exact opposite of how it had been with Adrian and Gillian.

Here were two people who really wanted the children and had no problem showing them affection and giving them cuddles.

'I can't put my finger on it,' I told Lisa. 'It just feels right.'

Of course, it helped that we knew all each other and, as Carol and I were friends, it made everything so much more relaxed. I think it rubbed off on the children, too.

After just over a week of to-ing and fro-ing, we agreed that the following Friday the children would move there permanently.

We arranged for us all to have dinner together at Carol's house and then the children would stay there permanently. There were no goodbye parties this time or any presents or cards. I took round the last of the children's things and then Liam made us all lasagne and garlic bread.

It was like any normal meal with friends with lots of laughter and chatter. But I could tell that the children were aware of the significance of this moment.

Dougie kept coming over and giving me extra cuddles and Sean kept glancing over at me as though seeking reassurance. Mary seemed very concerned about when she was going to next see me and Louisa.

'We will see you again, won't we, Louisa?' she asked her as we tucked into cheesecake for pudding.

'Of course you will, silly.' Louisa smiled. 'We're only round the corner and you can come and see us any time.

'Also, Mary, before I go tonight, I've got something very important I need to ask you.'

Mary's ears pricked up.

'What?' she gasped. 'What is it?'

'When Charlie and I get married next year I'd really like it if you would be my bridesmaid. Would that be OK?'

Mary looked stunned.

'Yes.' She nodded excitedly. Then she hesitated. 'But what does a bridesmaid mean?'

'It means that you get to wear a very pretty dress and you walk down the aisle with Louisa,' I explained. 'You only ask the most special people in your life, the ones you like the most, to be your bridesmaid.'

'It's a really, really important job,' Louisa told her. 'Do you think you can do it?'

Mary nodded eagerly, smiling from ear to ear.

Once we'd all finished dinner, I was keen for Louisa and me to head home. My belief was that goodbyes with the children should be brief and upbeat.

'Well, I think it's time Louisa and I were going,' I told them.

I gave them each a kiss and a big cuddle and Louisa did the same.

'I'll see you all very soon,' I promised.

Louisa and I walked home in silence, each of us processing our own thoughts.

'It's funny but I'm not as sad as normal,' she said at last. 'It doesn't really feel like they've gone. Seeing them there tonight, it just feels like they've always lived at Carol's house.'

'That's because it's right,' I told her. 'They're not leaving us. We're going to see them and they're still going to be part of our lives. That's the lovely thing about it.'

I did feel a deep sadness that I was no longer going to be the one tucking the children in at night, collecting them from school and comforting them when they fell over. But I didn't feel that overwhelming sense of grief that I get when a child leaves my home.

A couple of days later, I was just sorting through some washing when there was a knock at the door. I opened it to find Mary, Sean, Dougie and Carol standing there, grinning at me.

'I thought you lot had gone,' I laughed, hugging them tightly.

'We're very sorry to bother you, Maggie,' Carol said. 'Mary has lost her pink socks and her favourite spotty bow and she insisted that while we were passing we knocked on your door to see if she'd left them here.'

'Well it's very lucky that you did,' I said. 'Because I've just found a spotty bow in the bathroom and this morning I found a pair of pink socks stuffed down the side of the sofa!

'Do you want to come in for a coffee?' I asked Carol.

'Yes, if that's OK with you.' She nodded.

I opened the door and the children rushed in. Mary and Dougie plonked themselves in front of the telly and Sean got out the box of Lego while Carol and I had a cuppa and a Digestive.

'So how's it going?' I asked her.

'Really well,' she smiled. 'Don't get me wrong, there've been a few wobbles but nothing that we can't sort out. We're all still adjusting but overall I know we've done the right thing. We just feel so lucky to have them.'

We chatted for a while about this and that, until Dougie came wandering over to her.

'Can we go home now?' he asked. 'I'm starving.'

'Yes, of course, darling,' she told him.

'I bet you've got something really delicious for your tea, haven't you?' I smiled.

'Liam's made toad in the hole,' said Sean proudly. 'It's my favourite.'

'Right, that's it,' I joked. 'I'm getting my coat and coming round to your house.'

I waved them off and as I watched them skip down the street, hand in hand with Carol, my heart swelled with pride and happiness. It was such a different feeling from last time.

I always rely on my gut instinct. The feeling you get when adopters walk through your door is something that you can't describe. You just know if it's right. I had never had that feeling with Adrian and Gillian. Ultimately, they weren't horrible people at all; they just weren't ready to take on three damaged children with huge attachment and behavioural issues.

The odds had been stacked against the children because of their age and their behaviour and I'd felt so despondent when the adoption had failed. I couldn't have been happier now that they'd truly found their forever family.

Of course, I knew they would probably always have their insecurities because of the rejections that they'd suffered. Inevitably, over the years, they were going to have their ups and downs but I had total faith that Carol and Dave would be able to manage them. The children might have left my home, but in their place they had left me with a huge sense of pride and satisfaction and a heart full of joy and hope for the future.

As I settled down with a cup of tea, I rang Becky.

'I think it's high time you put me back on the available list,' I told her when she answered. 'I'm ready for my next placement.'

I couldn't wait to find out who that might be.

Epilogue

Much to my delight and relief, the children settled in well with Carol and Dave. I'd often see them walking past the house to and from school and sometimes they'd pop in for a juice and a biscuit, or Carol would invite Louisa and me round for dinner. We were like family friends and we were all very at ease and comfortable in each other's company. Inevitably, as the children got older, they had their ups and downs and Sean in particular would always struggle with school. But Carol and Dave gave them exactly what they needed – calm, consistency and love – and whatever issues came up, they got through them. I couldn't have hoped for better parents for the children and even though we had deliberately not presented Carol and Dave as their 'new mummy and daddy', it wasn't long before that's what all three children called them.

And as for Mary, you might be wondering how Louisa's wedding went and if she was a bridesmaid? Well, I'm afraid that's another story . . .

Acknowledgements

Thank you to my children, Tess, Pete and Sam, who are such a big part of my fostering today though I had not met you when Mary, Sean, Dougie and Louisa came into my home. To my wide circle of fostering friends – you know who you are – your support and your laughter are valued. To my friend Andrew B for your continued encouragement and care. Thanks also to Heather Bishop, who spent many hours listening and enabled this story to be told, my literary agent Rowan Lawton and to Anna Valentine at Trapeze for giving me the opportunity to share these stories.

A Note from Maggie

I really hope you enjoyed reading Mary, Sean and Dougie's stories. I love sharing my experiences of fostering with you, and I also love hearing what you think about them. If you enjoyed this book, or any of my others, please think about leaving a review online. I know other readers really benefit from your thoughts, and I do too.

To be the first to hear about my new books, you can keep in touch on my Facebook page @MaggieHartleyAuthor. I find it inspiring to learn about your own experiences of fostering and adoption, and to read your comments and reviews.

Finally, thank you so much for choosing to read *Denied a Mummy*. If you enjoyed it, there are others available including *Too Scared to Cry*, *Tiny Prisoners*, *The Little Ghost Girl*, *A Family for Christmas*, *Too Young to be a Mum*, *Who Will Love Me Now*, *The Girl No One Wanted*, *Battered, Broken, Healed*, *Is It My Fault Mummy?* and *Sold to be a Wife*. I hope you'll enjoy my next story just as much.

Maggie Hartley

Evie and Elliot are scrawny, filthy and wide-eyed with fear when they turn up on foster carer Maggie Hartley's doorstep. They're too afraid to leave the house and any intrusion of the outside world sends them into a panic. It's up to Maggie to unlock the truth of their heart-breaking upbringing, and to help them learn to smile again.

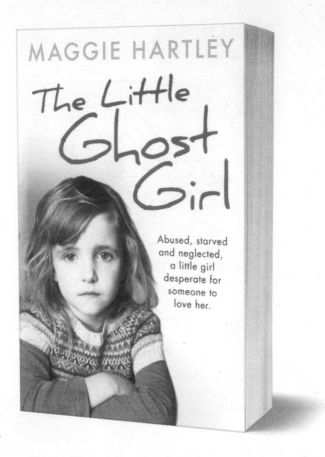

Ruth is a ghost of a girl when she arrives into foster mother Maggie Hartley's care. Pale, frail and withdrawn, it's clear to Maggie that Ruth had seen and experienced things that no 11-year-old should have to. Ruth is in desperate need of help, but can Maggie get through to her and unearth the harrowing secret she carries?

TOO YOUNG TO BE A MUM

When sixteen-year-old Jess arrives on foster carer Maggie Hartley's doorstep with her newborn son Jimmy, she has nowhere else to go. With social services threatening to take baby Jimmy into care, Jess knows that Maggie is her only chance of keeping her son. Can Maggie help Jess learn to become a mum?

WHO WILL LOVE ME NOW?

When ten-year-old Kirsty arrives at the home of foster carer Maggie Hartley, she is reeling from the rejection of her long-term foster family. She acts out, smashing up Maggie's home. But when she threatens to hurt the baby boy Maggie has fostered since birth, Maggie is placed in an impossible position; one that calls in to question her decision to become a foster carer in the first place...

BATTERED, BROKEN, HEALED

Six-week-old baby Jasmine comes to stay with Maggie after she is removed from her home. Neighbours have repeatedly called the police on suspicion of domestic violence, but her timid mother Hailey vehemently denies that anything is wrong. Can Maggie persuade Hailey to admit what's going on behind closed doors so that mother and baby can be reunited?

SOLD TO BE A WIFE

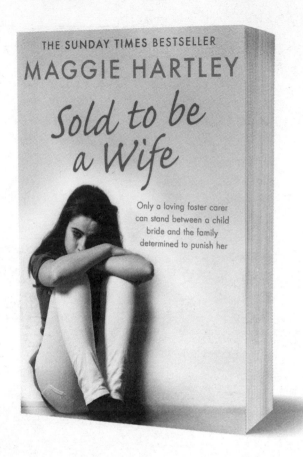

THE SUNDAY TIMES BESTSELLER
MAGGIE HARTLEY
Sold to be a Wife

Only a loving foster carer
can stand between a child
bride and the family
determined to punish her

Fourteen-year-old Shazia has been taken into care over a
fears that her family are planning to send her to Pakistan
for an arranged marriage. But with Shazia denying
everything and with social services unable to find any
evidence, Shazia is eventually allowed to return home. But
when Maggie wakes up a few weeks later in the middle of
the night to a call from the terrified Shazia, it looks like her
worst fears have been confirmed...

A baby too scared to cry. Two toddlers too scared to speak. This is the dramatic short story of three traumatised siblings, whose lives are transformed by the love of foster carer Maggie Hartley.

A FAMILY FOR CHRISTMAS

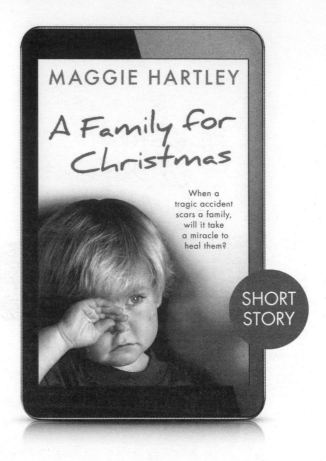

MAGGIE HARTLEY

A Family for Christmas

When a tragic accident scars a family, will it take a miracle to heal them?

SHORT STORY

A tragic accident leaves the life of toddler Edward changed forever and his family wracked with guilt. Will Maggie be able to help this family grieve for the son they've lost and learn to love the little boy he is now? And will Edward have a family to go home to at Christmas?

THE GIRL NO ONE WANTED

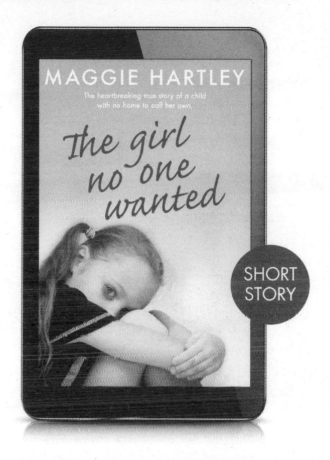

Eleven-year-old Leanne is out of control. With over forty placements in her short life, no local foster carers are willing to take in this angry and damaged little girl. Maggie is Leanne's only hope, and her last chance. If this placement fails, Leanne will have to be put in a secure unit. Where most others would simply walk away, Maggie refuses to give up on the little girl who's never known love.

IS IT MY FAULT MUMMY?

Seven-year-old Paris is trapped in a prison of guilt.
Devastated after the death of her baby brother, Joel,
Maggie faces one of the most heartbreaking cases yet as
she tries to break down the wall of guilt surrounding this
damaged little girl.